contents

computers & software
005 computers
015 software

industry
059 industrial parks
060 heavy industries
065 light industries
071 printing
075 paper making
078 energy
085 auto
087 electronics

management
089 public relations
092 marketing
096 consultation
110 information
112 human resources
113 headhunting

enterprise image
115 groups
125 industrial companies

high-technology industries
126 high-technology industries
135 research centers

architecture & real estate
140 architectural institutes
143 architectural projects
148 building
150 construction & decoration
152 real estate development
164 property management

transportation
166 conveyance
170 aviation
173 passenger liners

correspondence
177 telecommunications
188 express delivery companies

education
189 educational organizations
194 schools
205 training centers

sports
208 athletic meetings
210 sports competitions
214 athletic teams
220 sports centers
224 sports products

culture & art
226 art festivals
233 music & dance
237 theaters & art galleries

media
240 multimedia
246 television
253 movies
264 publishing houses
269 magazines
272 record labels
274 videos
275 disney

public services & government
279 government
286 communication centers

organizations
288 associations
301 international organizations
306 leagues

charity & commonwealth
308 charities
315 public welfare & environmental protection
317 foundations

NEW LOGO

A COLLECTION OF CORPORATE

IDENTITIES

NEW LOGO A COLLECTION OF CORPORATE IDENTITIES
2004 © PAGE ONE PUBLISHING PRIVATE LIMITED

Published in 2004 by
Page One Publishing Private Limited
20 Kaki Bukit View
Kaki Bukit Techpark II
Singapore 415956
Tel: (65) 6742-2088
Fax: (65) 6744-2088
enquiries@pageonegroup.com
www.pageonegroup.com

Distributed by:
Page One Publishing Private Limited
20 Kakit Bukit View
Kaki Bukit Techpark II
Singapore 415956
Tel: (65) 6742-2088
Fax: (65) 6744-2088

2004 © Liaoning Science and Technology Publishing House
Printed by SNP LeeFung Printers (Shen Zhen) Co.,Ltd
Chief Editor: Chen Ci Liang
Cover Design: Kelley Cheng, Meng Xinxin
Compiled by: Zhou Jianzhong, Feng Bin
Translator: Zhao Minchao
Format Design: Yin Jie
Examiner: Kang Qian, Jiang Lu

ISBN: 981-245-123-4

Printed in China

1
DIABLO COMPUTER

2
HITACHI DATA SYSTEMS

3
ATOMZ

4
HYPERSHELL INC

5
DISKCOPY

6
LOGITECH

7
INNOVATION DATA PROCESSING

1

4

DISKCOPY

5

Together, we **can** create miracles

2

Logitech®

6

Atomz

3

INNOVATION DATA PROCESSING

7

1

1
MEGAVIEW

2
SUN MICROSYSTEMS

3
DESKTOP RENEWAL 2000

4
PALM PDA

5
IBM

6
NCR

7
JONES DAY

2

5

3

6

4

7

1
LANTRONIX

2
POWER COMPUTING

3
CORPORATE SYSTEMS CENTER

4
INFORMATION FUSION

5
TCERT

6
TEAM DIGITS

7
AMD

LANTRONIX®

1

INFORMATION FUSION

4

2

Tcert
the power of Edapt™

5

Team Digits

Putting Technology in Your Hands

6

CSC

3

AMD

7

KLA Tencor

1

ANACOMP

2

A PC Professional
We make networks work.

3

roxio™

5

CSI
COMPUTER
SECURITY
INSTITUTE

6

KVK COMPUTERS

4

LatPro.com

7

1
KLATENCOR

2
ANACOMP

3
PC PROFESSIONAL

4
KVK COMPUTERS

5
ROXIO

6
COMPUTER SECURITY INSTITUTE

7
LAT PRO.COM

1
STOREASE.COM

2
MAIKON

3
IMATION

4
COMP USA PC

5
VERSATERM INC

6
DATA ARCHITECHS

7
OAK SYSTEMS

stor**ease**·com™

1

Formerly **BestWare**

2

5

IMATION

3

DATA ARCHITECHS

6

COMPUSA**PC**™

Custom Built for You™

4

7

1

5

1
DIANE STRONGWATER

2
NEC

3
APPLIED MATERIALS

4
LIEBERT

5
CDW

6
SAN DISK

7
VISTA SYSTEMS

8
TECH SHIELD

NEC

NEC Technologies

2

SanDisk

6

APPLIED MATERIALS®

INFORMATION FOR EVERYONE

3

VISTA
systems

7

Liebert®

4

TechShield

8

1
WESTERN DIGITAL

2
ICBIC

3
IOMEGA

4
PEOPLE SUPPORT

5
SPECTRUM COMPUTER SERVICES

6
NETWORK APPLIANCE

7
EMC

8
SUNDOG INTERACTIVE

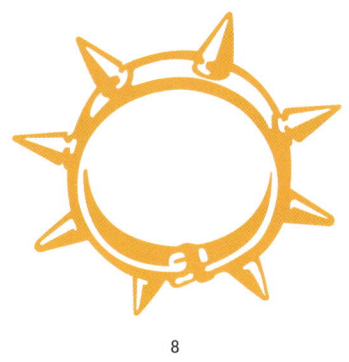

WESTERN DIGITAL
1

spectrum
COMPUTER SERVICES
5

ICBIC
2

NetworkAppliance®
6

iomega®
3

EMC²
THE STORAGE ARCHITECTS
7

PEOPLESUPPORT™
4

8

11

1

2

3

4

5

6

7

1
CEBIT 98 HANNOVER

2
KINGSTON TECHNOLOGY

3
COMPUTER CITY

4
WEB COM

5
INNOVATIVE COMPUTER
SYSTEMS INC.

6
HANDSPRING

7
DLP

1
MERCURY SYSTEMS

2
COMPUTER ASSOCIATES

3
ASPIRE BY ACER

4
POINT OF VIEW INC

5
SPECTR ALLIANCE

6
THE CAYENNE GROUP

7
CONTROL DATA

8
ASTRA DATA

MERCURY Systems
1

SpectrAlliance
5

COMPUTER ®
ASSOCIATES
Software superior by design.
2

thecayenne**group**
6

CONTROL DATA
7

aspire ™
by Acer
3

POINT OF VIEW INC.
4

ASTRA DATA
8

BRIDGEPOINT
I N T E R N A T I O N A L

1

FSI
flexicore systems, inc.

5

MAG

2

ICON

6

SanDisk

3

SyChip

4

FIT @ SUN

7

1
BRIDGE POINT INTERNATIONAL

2
MAG

3
SANDISK

4
SYCHIP

5
FSI FLEXICORE SYSTEMS, INC

6
ICON

7
SUN MICROSYSTEMS

1
OAK APTICAL

2
OAK WARP5

3
OAK AUDIO/COMM

1

2

3

CYBERPATH

SIMBA

zero G
SOFTWARE

io

GREAT PLAINS

sitraka

xmlsolutions

OBJECTIVE
EDGE INC

1
CYBERPATH

2
ZERO G SOFTWARE

3
GREAT PLAINS

4
XML SOLUTIONS

5
SIMBA

6
IO

7
SITRAKA

8
OBJECTIVE EDGE INC

1

5

2

6

3

7

4

8

1
MICROTEST

2
MOMENTUM SYSTEMS LIMITED

3
E LUSTRO ENTERPRISE EDITION

4
WHAT COUNTS

5
OMK

6
SOFTWARE SPECTRUM

7
DYNISCO

8
COMPLETE SOFTWARE SOLUT-
IONS

MICROTEST®

1

Manufacturing Knowledge

OMK GROUP ™

5

Momentum Systems Limited

2

SM

6

e**Lustro**
Enterprise Edition

3

7

WhatCounts

4

CSS
Complete Software Solutions

8

17

Cardiff Software™

1

connectME™

2

Autodesk Engineering

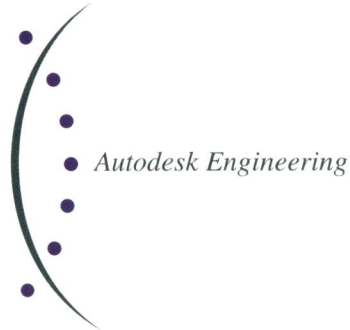

5

JavaOne℠

3

6

digital safe™

7

Levanta™

4

IMAGEMAKER
CD-R DUPLICATION SYSTEM

8

1
CARDIFF

2
CONNECT ME

3
JAVA ONE

4
LEVANTA

5
AUTODESK ENGINEERING

6
AUTODESK ENGINEERING

7
DIGITAL SAFE

8
MICROTECH CO INC/IMAGE MAKER

1
E TRACE

2
LEAP

3
SYQUEST

4
EXCHANGE SOFT

5
INFOCOM

6
BRICKHOUSE

7
NSI SOFTWARE

8
STORAGE APPS THE SMARTER AP-
PROACH

etrace
1

infocom
5

LEAP™
2

Brickhouse
6

SYQUEST®
3

NSI
SOFTWARE®
7

ExchangeSoft
4

StorageApps
The Smarter Approach™
8

19

MEMOTEC

1

TBI

5

NuMega ™

2

NetOp ®

6

S I G A B A ™

3

omgeo

7

katmango ™

4

autodessys INC

8

1
MEMOTEC

2
NUMEGA

3
SIGABA

4
KATMANGO

5
TBI

6
NETOP

7
OMGEO

8
AUTO DESSYS INC

1
ALPHABLOX

2
ILOG

3
SELF TEST SOFTWARE

4
QUICKLOGIC

5
GUARDED NET

6
INNER QUEST

7
TEL VISTA

alphablox™

1

QUICKLOGIC

4

ILOG

2

GUARDEDNET

5

Inner Quest

6

Self Test
SOFTWARE

3

TELvista℠

7

geek

4 3 3 5

1

NCSA

5

NEW FOCUS

2

eSpecto

6

BLUE MARTINI
S O F T W A R E

3

BLADE
SOFTWARE

7

TM
DATAFLUX

4

GREAT PLAINS®
S E E F A R T H E R

8

1
MILLER SQA

2
NEW FOCUS

3
BLUE MARTINI

4
DATA FLUX

5
NCSA

6
E SPECTO

7
BLADE SOFTWARE

8
GREAT PLAINS

1
VERTEX

2
STAR BASE

3
CLEAR CUBE TECHNOLOGY

4
CHILD & FAMILY PROFILE

5
ALEBRA

6
TELL-EUREKA

7
SIBLING SYSTEMS

8
EXPO DISC

vertex

1

ALEBRA™

5

starbase

2

Tell-Eureka

6

clearcube

3

7

CHILD & FAMILY PROFILE

4

ExpoDisc

8

T·H·QUEST

1

centegra™

5

™

2

agsoft™

6

WILLOWS
SOFTWARE

3

PINK

7

CONTIGO
SOFTWARE

4

WebTraffic.com

8

1
T.H.QUEST

2
ONLIVE!

3
WILLOWS SOFTWARE

4
CONTIGO

5
CENTEGRA

6
AGSOFT

7
PINK

8
WEB TRAFFIC.COM

1
NETWORK PHOTONICS

2
COMPUTER ASSOCIATES

3
POPKIN SOFTWARE

4
HOOKED ON PHONICS

5
ALEXSYS TEAM 2

6
OBJECT COMPUTING.INC

7
AUNGATE

Network Photonics

1

Computer Associates™

2

HOOKED ON
PHONICS

4

Alexsys
TEAM 2

5

POPKIN
S O F T W A R E

3

6

aungate
total communications management

7

TUMBLEWEED

1

eduPlan
software

2

USERNET99

3

CONVERGYS

4

PROVANCE

5

Satyam

6

QuantumShift™

7

1
TUMBLE WEED

2
EDUPLAN SOFTWARE

3
USER NET 99

4
CONVERGYS

5
PROVANCE

6
SATYAM

7
QUANTUM SHIFT

1
INTRAWARE

2
GOAHEAD SOFTWARE

3
XYLAN

4
SEJERSEN DIGITAL PROCESSING
SERVICES

5
BOMA

6
EXECUTIVE SOFTWARE

7
ONTOS

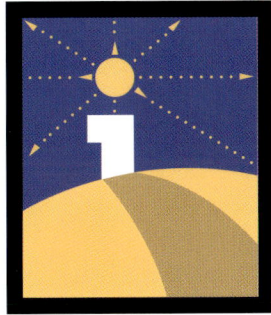

i n t r a w a r e

1

sdps

4

5

GOAHEAD

2

Executive®
Software

6

XYLAN

3

ONTOS

7

Veridicom

1

ShareWave™

5

ADEXA
KNOW MORE

2

INKTOMI
CORPORATION

6

3

NETSCREEN

7

requistitetechnology ™

4

WALLOP
SOFTWARE

8

1
VERIDICOM

2
ADEXA

3
ISPW

4
REQUISTITE TECHNOLOGY

5
SHARE WAVE

6
INKTOMI

7
NET SCREEN

8
WALLOP

1
GLIDES WEB TECHNOLOGY

2
CACHE

3
SNIA

4
SANA SECURITY

5
ONI SYSTEMS

6
QUALYS

7
SS&C

Sana Security

4

glides™

1

ONI Systems™

5

CACHÉ™

2

qualys

6

SNIA

3

7

Corporate Express

1

MAYAN™
Networks

5

PRIMAVERA

2

◯PTIMA™

6

x.eye

3

child
GUIDANCE

7

NightFire

4

Benchmark
Portal

8

1
CORPORATE EXPRESS

2
PRIMAVERA

3
X.EYE

4
NIGHT FIRE

5
MAYAN NETWORKS

6
PTIMA

7
CHILD GUIDANCE

8
BENCHMARK PORTAL

1
INTERCONNECT SERVICES INC

2
EMPOWER TEL

3
DIVERSIFIED SOFTWARE

4
N SITE SOFTWARE.INC

5
VALICERT

6
TROY SYSTEMS

7
VIALOG

8
CYPRESS

INTERCONNECT SERVICES, INC.

1

ValiCert®

5

empowerTel

2

6

Diversified Software

3

V I A L O G

7

nSite Software, Inc.

4

CYPRESS

8

ePeople^{SM}

1

SLEEPYCAT SOFTWARE
Makers of Berkeley DB

5

Hr
HyperRoll

2

TELISPARK

6

documentum

3

VUnet

7

DIGITAL PLANET™

4

LICENSE LOGIC

8

1
EPEOPLE

2
HYPER ROLL

3
DOCUMENTUM

4
DIGITAL PLANET

5
SLEEPYCAT SOFWARE MAKERS OF
BERKELEY DB

6
TELI SPARK

7
VALID LOGIC SYSTEMS

8
LICENSE LOGIC

1
AVANADE

2
STERLING DIGITAL

3
CHALLENGER SYSTEMS.INC.

4
SARANAC SOFTWARE.INC

5
ESPRESSO WEB

6
IMPROV ASYLUM

7
IMODE RETRIEVAL SYSTEMS

avanade℠
1

saranac
SOFTWARE, INC.
4

BirdSight
2

espressoWeb.com
5

Improv Asylum
6

Challenger
SYSTEMS, INC.
3

imode
retrieval systems
7

33

portalplayer

1

Visteon

5

STSN

2

Syntegra

6

SYNETICS

4

GENERATOR
DIGITAL POST PRODUCTION

7

3

1
PORTAL PLAYER

2
STSN

3
PROFIT MASTER CANADA

4
SYNETICS

5
VISTEON

6
SYNTEGRA

7
GENERATOR DIGITAL POST P-
RODUCTION

1
KEYWARE

2
SHARE

3
BUSINESS OBJECTS

4
DIFFUSION

5
FXALL

6
LAVA STORM

7
TRANS 2000

8
VOICE EXCHANGE

KeyWare™

1

S H A R E

2

BUSINESS OBJECTS ®

3

D I F F U S I O N

4

FXall®

5

lava™ **STORM**

6

TRANS™ **2000**

7

VOEX VOICE EXCHANGE

8

35

Brooktrout®

1

SpartaCom®

2

Cerebellum
SOFTWARE

3

Storage WOrks™
Solutions from Digital Equipment Corporation

4

COMVERSE

5

EMBARCADERO
TECHNOLOGIES®

6

GUARDENT℠
secure digital infrastructure

7

R S A
Rochester Software Associates, Inc
Digital Document Software Solutions

8

Sapient™

9

1
BROOKTROUT

2
SPARTA COM

3
CEREBELLUM SOFTWARE

4
STORAGE WORKS

5
COMVERSE

6
EMBARCADERO TECHNOLOGIES

7
GUARDENT SECURE DIGITAL INF-
RASTRUCTURE

8
ROCHESTER SOFTWARE ASSOCIAT-
ES INC

9
SAPIENT

1
ENX

2
VISARA INTERMATIONAL

3
VERVE

4
CONNX SOLUTIONS

5
SGF (SPECIALTIES GRAPHIC FIN-
SHERS)

6
CENTURY

7
APP GENESYS

8
FAIR COM

9
EMAIL XTENDER

1

6

2

7

3

4

8

5

9

1

2

Simplex

3

VALORSYSTEMS

4

5

3D PRO

6

NOMADIX™

7

TeamPlay
IY PROJECT MANAGEMENT SOFTWARE

8

pulse

9

1
CACHEFLOW

2
ISOGON

3
SIMPLEX

4
VALOR SYSTEMS

5
ROGUE WAVE

6
3D PRO

7
NOMADIX

8
TEAM PLAY

9
PULSE SYSTEMS INC

1
BREW CUSTOMIZE.PERSONALIZE.
REALIZE

2
Z FRAME

3
METAVANTE

4
BLUE SOCKET

5
Enroute

6
1997 BEST NEW OT PRODUCT

7
GALIL

8
ALVION TECHNOLOGIES

enroute

brew™
Customize. Personalize. Realize.™

1

zFrame™

2

1997
BEST
NEW
OT
PRODUCT

OBJECT
WORLD

6

Metavante

3

GALIL
WE MOVE THE WORLD

7

bluesocket

4

ALVION

8

GETNETHITS
TARGETED TRAFFIC, delivered.

1

ICEBERG

2

STARWAVE

3

✉✉✉ **Communiqué**

4

MAILBOY MAILBOY MAILBOY MAILBOY MAILBOY

5

DX3™

6

CoNet
Email in detail.

7

Dreamer

8

1
GET NET HITS

2
ICEBERG

3
STARWAVE

4
COMMUNIQUE

5
MAILBOY

6
DX3

7
CNET

8
DREAMER SOFTWARE ENGINEERING

1
EXCEL

2
EXCEL

3
MICROSOFT

4
EXCEL

5
MICROSOFT

6
MICROSOFT CORPORATION

7
MICROSOFT

8
MICROSOFT

1

TalkOn

5

$$E = MS^2$$

6

2

3

ultimateTV™

7

EXCELebrate
2000

4

TalkOn

8

TOPSPIN®

1

MQSoftware
QNami!™

2

EMC²

VELOCITY²
PARTNER
PROGRAM

5

SpeechWorks

3

dataedge SM
► SOLUTIONS

6

MagniFire

4

TAKEFIVE
SOFTWARE

7

1
TOPSPIN

2
MQ SOFTWARE

3
SPEECH WORKS

4
MAGNI FIRE

5
EMC

6
DATA EDGE

7
TAKE FIVE SOFTWARE

1
THE MEASUREMENT FACTORY

2
CALYPSO

3
OTG SOFTWARE

4
TOTAL SYSTEM SERVICES

5
KOREA PROGRAMMED INSTRUCTION

6
MAKO SOFTWARE

7
BEEHIVE SYSTEMS

THE MEASUREMENT FACTORY

1

CALYPSO®
e-mail

2

otg
SOFTWARE

3

MAKO

6

DOTSCONNECT

4

beehivesystems

7

TechSpace

1

1
TECH SPACE

2
SENDMAIL

3
COPPER MOUNTAIN

4
TWELVE HORSES

5
BREAKAWAY TECHNOLOGIES

6
ACCESSEDGE

7
ITAA

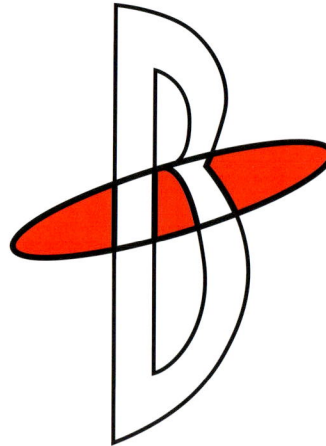

BREAKAWAY TECHNOLOGIES

5

SENDMAIL ®

2

COPPER MOUNTAIN

3

ACCESSEDGE

6

TWELVE HORSES

4

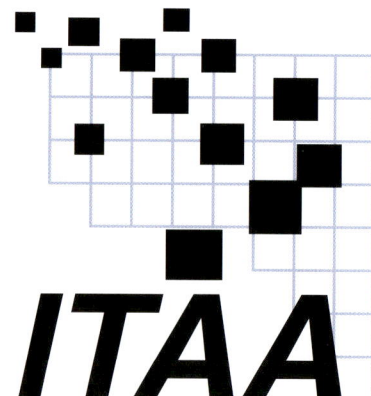

ITAA

7

1
ZILLIANT

2
ARGENESIS

3
CORE SOFTEWARE

4
INTRUSION.COM

5
SURF CONTROL

6
SQUIRES

7
SPEED LINK

4

1

5

2

6

3

7

Bluesoft Inc.

1

GENEVA software

2

MOTIF, INC.

3

OPTIKA

4

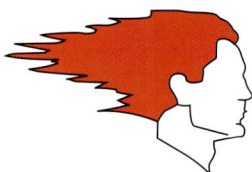 **fusionstorm**

5

6

COPPER COMPATIBLE TM

7

c a p s t a n

8

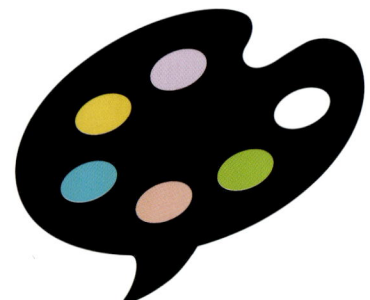

9

1
BLUESOFT INC

2
GENEVA SOFTWARE

3
MOTIF INC.

4
OPTIKA

5
FUSIONSTORM

6
BOCAVISION

7
COPPER COMPATIBLE

8
CAPSTAN

9
ART OF SPEECH

1
PRINT IMAGE MATCHING

2
LEGATO

3
ETEAMZ

4
CURRICULA

5
METEX SYSTEMS INC

6
BETA SYSTEMS

7
INTEGRATED

8
NEOHAPSIS

PRINT Image Matching™

1

METEX SYSTEMS INC.

SOFTWARE DEVELOPMENT

5

LEGATO™

2

BETA systems

6

e teamz

3

integrated

7

CURRICULA

4

NEOHAPSIS

8

47

Pathlore

1

PEOPLE Soft ®

5

real ™

2

Always Reaching Higher

src

6

ПUΛ

3

bea ™

7

TM1 ™
SOFTWARE

4

SuSE

8

1
PATHLORE SOFTWARE CORP

2
REALPLAY

3
NUA

4
TM1

5
PEOPLE SOFT

6
SRC

7
BEA

8
SUSE

1
SYMBIOS

2
VIGILANTE

3
PERSONAL LIDRARY SOFTWARE

4
POET SOFTWARE

5
CONCEPT INTERACTIVE.INC

6
ASYMETRIX CORPORATION

7
ULTI VERSE

8
ASYMETRIX

SYMBIOS
L O G I C ™

1

TOOLBOOK
APPLICATION

6

VIGILANTe

2

PLS

3

UltiVerse

7

POET
S O F T W A R E

4

5

ASYMETRIX
LEARNING SYSTEMS, INC.

8

PriceRadar.com™

1

COMPREHENSIVE
SOFTWARE SYSTEMS™

2

Cornerstone Systems, Inc.

3

DAI

4

TREND
M I C R C O

5

GATORS'

6

7

agillion

8

1
PRICE RADAR.COM

2
COMPREHENSIVE SOFTWARE SYS-
TEMS

3
CORNERSTONE SYSTEMS
INC.

4
DEVELOPMENT ALTERMAT IVES I-
NC

5
TREND MICRCO

6
GATORS

7
PACKAGE SOFTWARE

8
AGILLION

1
CONNEXT

2
MONTAVISTA

3
ONYX SOFTWARE

4
SAPIENT CORPORATION

5
REMEDY CORPORATION

6
BMC SOFTWARE

7
PROTOCOM DEVELOPMENT SYSTEMS

8
COREL

CONNEXT ®

1

bmcsoftware

6

MONTAVISTA

2

ONYX

3

Protocom
Development Systems

7

Sapient

4

Remedy ®
Corporation

5

COREL ®

8

Cayenta

1

tdwi
THE DATA WAREHOUSING INSTITUTE

2

SL
Sherrill-Lubinski

5

6

PURE ATRIA

3

Streamaster

7

a division of

IMC
Interactive Multimedia
Corporation

4

SQA®

8

1
CAYENTA A TITAN COMPANY

2
TDWI THE DATA WAREHOUSING I-
NSTITUTE

3
PURE ATRIA

4
IMC

5
SHERRILL-LUBINSKI

6
ENTOMO

7
STREAMASTER

8
SQA

1
ZERO G

2
ICL A FUJITSU COMPANY

3
WEB SENSE

4
IGROUP

5
ALERT PAGE

6
E LETTER

7
EPICOR

8
MAGIC

AlertPage™

E N T E R P R I S E

5

ZERO G

1

iCL

a Fujitsu company

2

E letter®

A S D I R E C T A S Y O U C A N G E T

6

WEBSENSE

3

epicor™

7

igroup

4

MAGIC

8

VINCA®

1

LSI LOGIC®

STORAGE SYSTEMS

6

SYBASE

2

Precise

3

CSI

7

ssh®

COMMUNICATIONS SECURITY

8

ISOCOR®

4

5

9

1
VINCA

2
SYBASE

3
PRECISE

4
ISOCOR

5
SEAGATE SOFTWARE

6
LSILOGIC

7
CSI

8
SSH COMMUNICATIONS SECURITY

9
QUADBASE SYSTEMS.INC.

1
XL SYSTEMS

2
STERLING COMMERCE

3
INTUIT

4 .
TECH FI

5
PILOT SOFTWARE

6
DQE

7
KUBIX LTD

8
MCAFEE SECURITY

9
VISIONTEK

Pilot
SOFTWARE

5

1

DQE sm

6

STERLING
COMMERCE

2

KUBIX

7

Intuit ®

3

McAfee
SECURITY

8

techfi

4

visiontek ™

9

pandesic™

1

DataCore
S O F T W A R E

2

W FEX

3

CompTIA®

4

dbaDIRECT

5

Vigilinx
Digital Security Solutions

6

COGNOS

7

8

1
PANDESIC

2
DATA CORE SOFTWARE

3
WOFEX

4
COMP TIA

5
DBA DIRECT

6
VIGILINX DIGITAL SECURITY
SOLUTIONS

7
COGNOS

8
ANALYTIX PITTSBURGH

1
AONIX

2
COREL

3
DOUBLE CLICK

4
CITRIX

5
INFOMAGIC

6
ASCENTIAL SOFTWARE

7
FINANCEWARE.COM

8
OBJECT SWITCH

InfoMagic
5

Aonix
1

Ascential™
Software
6

COREL™
2

financeware ● com
7

DoubleClick
3

CITRIX®
4

ObjectSwitch
8

DataVantage®

1

TIBCO

2

ORACLE®
SOFTWARE POWERS THE INTERNET ™

3

EMPRESS
SOFTWARE INC.

4

iLAB

5

SCANTRON®

6

im

7

VIVATO

8

Rational®

9

1
DATA VANTAGE SEIZE THE DATA

2
TIBCO

3
ORACLE SOFTWARE POWERS THE
INTERNET

4
EMPRESS

5
ILAB

6
SCANTRON

7
INTERNET MANAGER

8
VIVATO

9
RATIONAL

1
CENTRAL PARK CORPORATE CA-
MPUS

2
NORTHERN IRELAND

3
SHORELINE TECHNOLOGY PARK

4
THE DRIVE

5
PORT COLUMBUS EXECUTIVE PARK

6
BIO BELT

7
SOUTHERN ASSOCIATES CORPORATE
CENTER

CENTRAL PARK
CORPORATE CAMPUS

1

NorthernIreland
fresh talent at work

2

SHORELINE
TECHNOLOGY PARK

3

5

BioBelt
SM

6

the corporate park
drive

4

Southern Associates
Corporate Center

7

59

ANDERSON MANUFACTURING

1

ALCOA

2

industrial metal

5

ARTEC MACHINE SYSTEMS

3

6

CATERPILLAR®

4

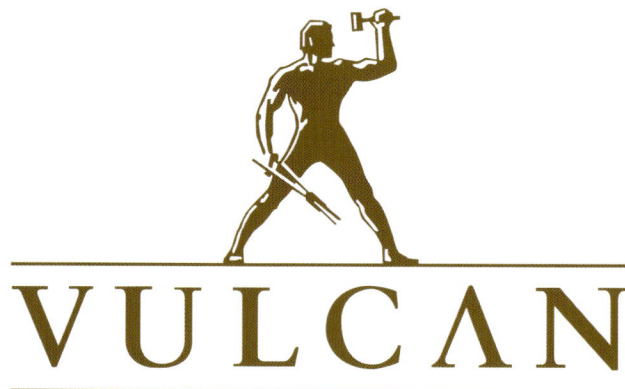

7

1
ANDERSON MANUFACTURING

2
ALCOA

3
ARTEC MACHINE SYSTEMS

4
CATERPILLAR

5
INDUSTRIAL METAL

6
SHIMANO

7
VULCAN

1
EMF EVAPORATED METAL FILMS

2
BOEING

3
TAYLOR MADE TUNGSTEN.STEEL

4
FROSTAD ATEILER

5
WARTSILA NSD CORPORATION

6
ALLEN'S EXCAVATING

7
LRON EASEL

8
EFG COMPANIES

1

2

3

4

WÄRTSILÄ NSD

5

6

7

8

KYOCERA

1

Rockwell

2

CONTINENTAL DIVIDE

TRAIL ALLIANCE

3

S A N S U I

5

GEAR

6

**OPTICAL
SYNERGY**
I N C

7

Pinnacle

DECISION SYSTEMS, INC

4

8

1
KYOCERA

2
ROCKWELL

3
CONTINENTAL DIVIDE TRAIL
ALLIANCE

4
PINNACLE

5
SANSUI INDUSTRY

6
FIN GEAR

7
OPTICAL SYNERGY.INC

8
AVNET

1
MEGAFAB

2
SYSTEMS MANUFACTURING CORP-
ORATION

3
PILLSBURY WINTHROP

4
ADVANCED MACHINING.INC

5
AUTONOMY

6
RALEIGH CYCLE COMPANY OF AM-
ERICA

7
ACCUTEC USA

8
TOMAGO ALUMINIUM

Autonomy

5

1

6

SMC Systems Manufacturing Corporation

2

ACCUTEC USA

7

PILLSBURY WINTHROP LLP

3

Advanced MACHINING, INC

4

8

UNIGEN

1

KOSCO

5

2

CLOROX

6

4j

7

allium
laboratorios sl

3

averda

4

SHIMANO®

8

1
UNIGEN

2
SOLUTIA

3
ALLIUM LABORATORIOS

4
AVERDA

5
KOREA STEEL CHEMICAL CO.LTD

6
CLOROX

7
4J CHEMICALS LLC

8
SHIMANO

1
GLOBAL PRINT RUNNER

2
OCE

3
ECOWATER SYSTEMS

4
WETZONE WAVEGAMES

5
TSUNAMI DIVE GEAR

6
DEEP DESIRE

7
KENMORE

8
PREAMBLE INSTRUMENTS

1

TSUNAMI DIVE GEAR

5

océ

2

DeepDesire

6

ECOWATER S Y S T E M S ®

3

Kenmore

7

WetZone WAVEGAMES

4

PREAMBLE INSTRUMENTS

8

MIGCO
IRRIGATION SYSTEMS

1

2

doormation

5

3

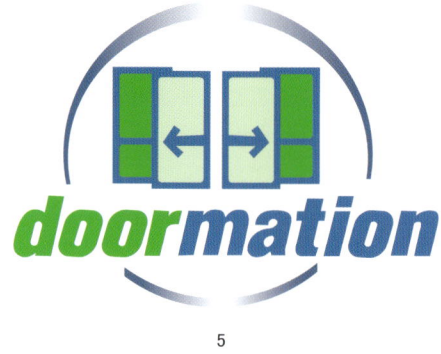

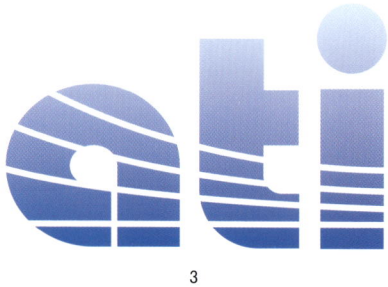

Rugged 600 Polyester

6

BUBBLE MACHINE
MOBILE PRESSURE WASH AND DETAIL

4

TRANSWORLD
LUBRICANTS, INC.

7

1
MIGCO IRRIGATION SYSTEMS

2
SANDFORD COLOR CORPORATION

3
ATI

4
BUBBLE MACHINE

5
DOOR MATION

6
RUGGED 600 POLYESTER

7
TRANS WORLD LUBRICANTS.INC.

1
NATIONAL BICYCLE REPLACEMENT
COMPANY

2
QUALITY REFRIGERATION

3
TEXAS INSTRUMENTS

4
RAINBOW DIRECT SERIOUS SW-
INGSETS & KIDS STUFF

5
ACOUSTIC SOUNDS INC.

6
HEARTH AND HOME

7
YOKOHAMA

8
ULTIMATE BODY SCAN

1

ACOUSTIC SOUNDS INC.

5

2

6

TEXAS INSTRUMENTS

3

YOKOHAMA

7

RAINBOWDIRECT
Serious Swingsets & Kids Stuff

4

ULTIMATE
BODY SCAN

8

1

2

5

6

3

7

8

4

9

1
ANVI VENDING

2
RACK SPACE MANAGED HOSTING

3
SONOCO

4
TRUE SPECTRA

5
THE HAYES COMPANY INC

6
OCEAN FOX DIVE SHOP

7
SHOWER HEAD

8
THE PHENIX OPTICAL CO

9
SMARTSHIELD SUNSCREENS.LTD

1
PFRIMMER

2
RELIABLE HEATING AND COOLING

3
IM—LAB

4
THE KITCHEN

5
VIS.TECH

6
DANVILLE TENT & AWNING

7
REI

8
BAUMS CO.,LTD ENGINEERING FIRM

9
THERA GAMES

1

American Pavilion

6

2

7

IM-LAB

3

4

BAUMS

8

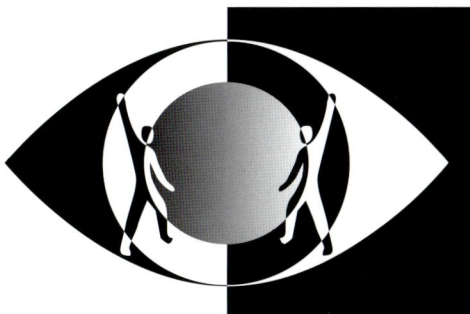

5

Thera Games™

9

1

2

3

4

5

6

7

8

1
PUR

2
LOWEPRO

3
PHONAK

4
MARTIN MARIOTTA MATERIALS

5
ILLUMENO LIGHTINGS

6
ROGERS GLASS WORKS

7
MARUBENI PLAX CORPERATION

8
KITCHEN DIMENSIONS

1
BASS LITHO

2
BLUE DUCK

3
CURRENT

4
MC CORD PRINTING

5
COLORSCAN DALLAS

6
PEGASUS IMAGING CORPORATION

Current ®

3

1

McCORD PRINTING

4

Blue Duck
SCREEN   PRINTING

2

5

PEGASUS IMAGING CORPORATION

6

71

Preferred
SOLUTIONS INPRINT

1

Roll Systems
non-stop printing

2

3

4

5

6

7

1
PREFERRED

2
ROLL SYSTEMS NON-STOP PRIN-
TING

3
ANDERSON PRINTING

4
HUTCHISON ALLGOOD PRINTING

5
CREATIVE PRINTING

6
LIBERTY PRINTING COMPANY

7
KOHLER AND SONS PRINTING CO-
MPANY

1
THE PRINT COMPANY

2
MASTER PRINTING

3
ANDERSON LITHOGRAPH

4
STANDARD PRINTING

5
INTERNATIONAL ASSOCIATION OF
PRINTING HOUSE GRAFTSMEN

6
ATLAS COLOR IMAGING

7
LAMB PRINT

The PRINT Company

established 1971

1

4

5

master printing

2

6

Anderson Lithograph

3

7

1

1
BUCHANAN PRINTING

2
KROMA LITHOGRAPHERS INC

3
PHARMA PRINT

4
WILLIAM CHARLES PRINTING C-
OMPANY

5
ROYAL GRAPHICS

6
TRI COMPANY

ROYAL ™

GRAPHICS

5

2

Pharma **Print**

3

tri company

6

WILLIAM CHARLES PRINTING COMPANY

4

WEST LINN PAPER COMPANY

APPLETON PAPERS

1

International Paper

2

1
APPLETON PAPERS

2
INTERNATIONAL PAPER

3
FOX RIVER PAPER CO

4
GEORGIA-PACIFIC PAPERS

5
BECKETT PAPER

6
POTLATCH

7
WAUSAU PAPERS

5

FOX RIVER® PAPER CO
SIMPSON

3

Potlatch

6

Georgia-Pacific Papers

4

wausau papers

7

1
RICE PAPER INC

2
PAPER SOURCE HAWAII

3
GREEN/HEIWA PAPER CO.LTD

4
PROVINCLAL PAPERS

5
SPAR

6
BLUE RIDGE PAPER PRODUCTS
INC

7
NORSKE SKOG

8
HEIWA PAPER CO.LTD

SPAR

5

RICE PAPER

1

PaperSource

2

3

6

7

PROVINCLAL
PAPERS

4

h   i w a

8

AEP AMERICAN® ELECTRIC POWER

1

ALSTOM

2

Manitowoc

3

4

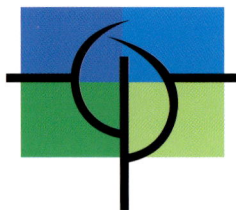

GREAT PLAINS ENERGY℠

5

Beacon POWER™

6

Hpower®

7

SOUTHERN COMPANY

8

1
AMERICAN ELECTRIC POWER

2
ALSTOM

3
MANITOWOC

4
VAEST

5
GREAT PLAINS ENERGY

6
BEACON POWER

7
HPOWER

8
SOUTHERN COMPANY

1
DOMINION

2
LENANG MURNI

3
SAN DIEGO GAS & ELECTRIC

4
LA LUNA OIL COMPANY

5
SUPERIOR ENERGY LLC

6
SOUTHERN CALIFORNIA GAS CO-
MPANY

7
ENRON

Dominion

1

4

LENANG MURNI

2

Superior Energy LLC

5

6

3

7

CINERGY ®

1

1
CINERGY

2
SEMPRA ENERGY

3
UNITED UTILITIES

4
TEXCO

5
SOUTHERN CALIFORNIA GAS CO-
MPANY

6
PALO ALTO UTILITIES

7
CIT

Southern California Gas Company

5

Sempra Energy®

2

United Utilities

3

6

 A WORLD OF ENERGY℠

4

cit

7

1
CON EDISON

2
METALIA

3
BEXARMET WATER DISTRIC

4
THERMA LINK

5
ACE GROUP

6
ATLAS OIL

7
SOQUEL CREEK WATER DISTRICT

8
COLUMBIA ENERGY GROUP

conEdison

1

5

2

ACESM

6

BexarMet
W A T E R   D I S T R I C

3

**SOQUEL
CREEK
WATER
DISTRICT**

7

ThermaLink™

4

**Columbia
Energy
Group**SM

8

ALLIANT ENERGY
Resources

1

BOLT

5

ConocoPhillips

2

PEM

PACIFIC ENERGY
MANAGEMENT COMPANY

6

P·M·R

PRINCETON MANAGEMENT RESOURCES, INC.

3

Mobil

4

7

1
ALLIANT ENERGY RESOURCES

2
CONOCO PHILLIPS

3
PMR

4
MOBIL

5
BOLT

6
PACIFIC ENERGY MANAGEMENT
COMPANY

7
U.S. DEPARTMENT OF ENERGY

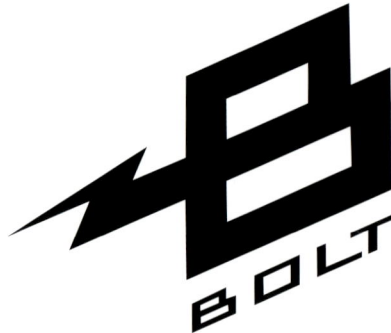

1
TAIHEIYO SEKIYU

2
HIGH PLAINS ENERGY

3
GREEN MOUNTAIN ENERGY PART-
NERS

4
PULSE UNITED ENERGY

5
BP

6
DYNEGY

7
MITSUI SEKKA

pulse
united energy

4

太平洋石油
TAIHEIYO OIL

1

bp

5

2

DYNEGY

6

Green Mountain
Energy Partners

3

三井石化

7

1

HYDRATECH

2

3

4
Aquila

viacore

5

A

6

7

8

1
GEORGIA POWER COMPANY

2
HYDRA TECH INC

3
HYDRA TECH

4
A QUILA

5
VIACORE

6
ATLAS OIL

7
HACKENY

8
OTAKI GAS

1
JEEP

2
DODGE

3
THE SPIRIT OF ISUZU

4
THE GILLETTE COMPANY

5
FIREWHEEL AUTOMOTIVE

6
SAAB

7
SATURN

ONLY INA

Jeep®

1

4

2

5

6

3

7

1

AQUARIAN BICYCLES
5

Steel-Horse
M O T O R C Y C L E   C O
2

6

THUNDER
INTO THE NEXT CENTURY
3

axis
MOTORCYCLES
7

AZUMA™
4

YASKAWA
Energy In Motion™
8

1
MIRROR MOUNTAIN MOTORCYCLES

2
STEEL HORSE MOTORCYCLE CO

3
THUNDER INTO THE NEXT CENTURY HARLEY DAVIDSON

4
AZUMA

5
AQUARIAN BICYCLES

6
ROTWILD

7
AXIS MOTORCYCLES

8
YASKAWA

1
TOSHIBA EID

2
NK

3
NATIONAL SEMICONDUCTOR

4
SENSORMATIC

5
NIMAX

6
NOVELLUS

7
TELECHECK

FYI

1

Nimax
AUTOID • POS SOLUTIONS

5

NK

2

NOVELLUS

6

National Semiconductor

3

Eclipse™

7

® **Sensormatic**
WORLD LEADER IN ELECTRONIC SECURITY

4

NEW LOGO industry

Cyrix®

1

ISOPIA

2

SAMSUNG CONTACT

3

DIGITAL iMAGER™

4

ADDTRON®

5

LAMBDA Electronics Inc. λ

6

 **ETK** ELEKTRO / TECHNIK / KAPPACHER

7

OBJECTIVE SYSTEMS INTEGRATORS

8

1
CYRIX

2
ISOPIA

3
SAMSUNG CONTACT

4
DIGITAL IMAGER

5
ADDTRON

6
LAMBDA

7
ETK/ELEKTRO TECHNIK KAPPACHER

8
OBJECTIVE SYSTEMS INTEGRATORS

1
FACE TIME

2
ZONE

3
AESTIX

4
WHALE COMMUNICATIONS

5
HEINZ COMMUNICATIONS

6
MARHOEFER COMMUNICATIONS

7
DIVA

8
NEWPORT COMMUNICATIONS

9
ASTRACHAN COMMUNICATIONS

FACE TIME

1

5

zone
communications

2

6

aestix

3

DIVA™

7

8

Whale
Communications®

4

AWOLPET
.COM

9

PRECISE PUBLIC RELATIONS

somethings are *better* said.

1

1
PRECISE PUBLIC RELATIONS

2
INTER ACTIVE PUBLIC RELATIONS

3
WDG COMMUNICATIONS

4
BLISS EVENTS

5
CROSSROADS COMMUNICATIONS

6
COMMUNICATION CONCEPTS.INC

7
OMNI SOURCE

8
Crossroads Communications

InterActive

PUBLIC RELATIONS

2

5

6

3

OmniSource

7

Bliss

EVENTS

4

shipmates

8

1
CHRYSLER CORPORATION COMMU-
NICATIONS GROUP

2
GS DESIGN INC

3
SPRING DOT

4
SUN UP MARKETING COMMUNICAT-
IONS

5
DAVOL COMMUNICATIONS

6
POARITY

7
MRV COMMUNICATIONS.INC.

8
AERIAL

1

DAVOL

5

2

6

SpringDot™
ENERGIZED
COMMUNICATION

3

MRV
Communications, Inc.

7

SunUp
MARKETING
COMMUNICATIONS

4

Aerial SM
COMMUNICATIONS

8

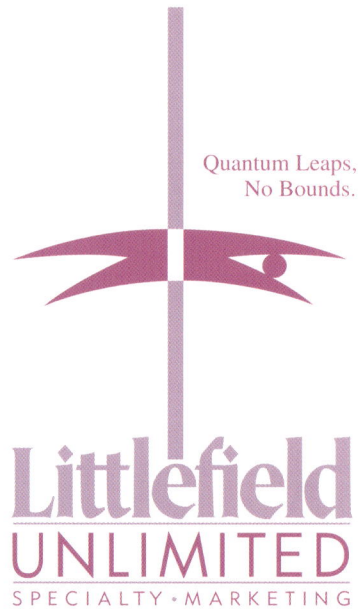

E Ray
PROMOTIONS

1

RIVER
MARKETING, INC.

5

2

Quantum Leaps,
No Bounds.

Littlefield
UNLIMITED
SPECIALTY · MARKETING

6

ibc
Interactive Brand Center

3

4

TM

TRIANGLE MLS
MULTIPLE LISTING SERVICES

7

1
E RAY PROMOTIONS

2
DRANEY TELEMARKETING

3
IBC

4
K/C/E MARKEING SERVICES

5
RIVER MARKETING.INC

6
LITTLEFIELD UNLIMITED

7
TRIANGLE MLS MULTIPLE LIST-
ING SERVICES

1
BRAND SYNERGY

2
WOLPER SALES AGENCY

3
EAR TO EAR

4
HUNGRY MINDS

5
BRANDABLE ONLINE.COM

6
RETURNS ONLINE

7
IVIE & ASSOCIATES.INC

8
EMERGE SMART

BRAND
SYNERGY

1

BRANDABLE
online.com

5

2

returns online

6

EAR TO EAR

3

IVIE & ASSOCIATES, INC.
MARKETING COMMUNICATIONS

7

Hungry Minds™

4

emergesmart

8

1
DESIGN IMAGE COMMUNICATIONS

2
67 WINE & SPIRITS INC

3
TO THE POINT

4
NEW BAND HORIZONS

5
THINK NEW IDEAS INC

6
MADISON ASSET MARKETPLACE

7
CONSUME EVOLUTION

1

GSM
GLOBAL NETWORK℠

5

67
67 Wine & Spirits INC
S I N C E   1 9 4 1

2

TO THE POINT

3

Madison
ASSET MARKETPLACE

6

New Band Horizons

4

7

1
GLOBAL MARKETING SYSTEMS

2
WEST ASSOCIATES

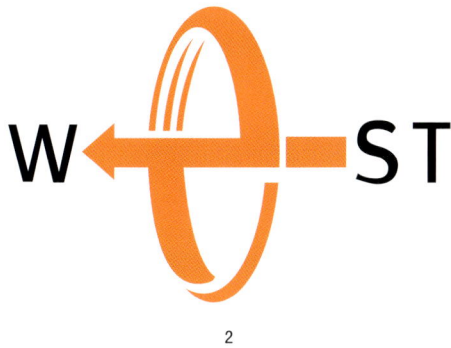

3
END POINTS INC

4
CUTLER TRAVEL MARKETING

5
SEEKERS

6
PRO MOTION

7
ENSEMBLE INC

8
BRANDOLOGY

GMS

1

5

PRO MOTION

6

W-ST

2

EndPoints

3

ENSEMBLE

7

CTM

4

Brandology
Marketing Consulting

8

Manugistics®

1

2

inner circle

3

BE | CENTRIC

4

FORTIS

5

MindTree
CONSULTING

6

Project
Liberty
Feel free
to feel better

7

1
MANUGISTICS

2
ALKA JOSHI MARKETING

3
INNER CIRCLE

4
BE CENTRIC

5
FORTIS

6
MIND TREE CONSULTING

7
PROJECT LIBERTY

1
PLAUT CONSULTING

2
ANSWER THINK

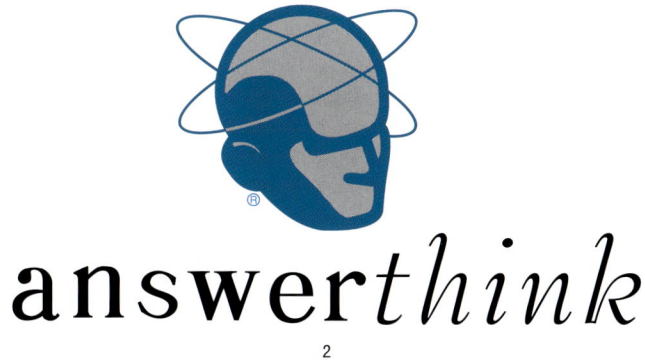

3
TECH-POINT

4
"4" CLICKS SOLUTIONS

5
RAW INNOVATIONS

6
ELM RIDGE VALUE ADVISORS

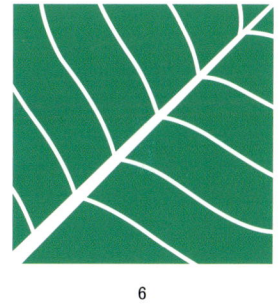

7
BLUE STORM

8
UNIVERSAL ADVISORY SERVICES, INC

PLAUT

1

RAW
INNOVATIONS

5

answerthink

2

6

3

BlueStorm

7

Clicks Solutions™

4

8

BUTLER
International

1

Global Entrepolis
@ Singapore

2

SPG

5

3

PIECE of **pie**
Marketing

7

kitcole™
investment advisory services

4

Global Knowledge

8

1
BUTLER INTERNATIONAL

2
GLOBAL ENTREPOLIS SINGAPORE

3
DONNELLEY ENTERPRISE SOLUT-
IONS

4
KITCOLE

5
SOLUTIONS PLANNING GROUP

6
PERSONA PRINCIPLE

7
PIECE OF PIE MARKETING

8
GLOBAL KNOWLEDGE

6

1
ASTERISK

2
RHI ROBERT HALF INTERNATIONAL INC.

3
WHY MEN ARE ?

4
TOWER GROUP

5
SCHOLARSHIP SURETY.INC

6
CHARITABLE IRA.LLC

7
ERRAND BEES

asterisk

1

TOWERGROUPsm

4

RHI

2

5

WHY MEN ARE

3

Charitable IRA,LLC
The New Leader in Endowments

6

7

Business Layers™

1

fsp
THZNK
OPERATE
BUILD

2

COMPUTERGISTICS L.L.C.

3

SA
Service Advisors

4

coach berry™
EOUCATION & SPORTS CONSULTING

5

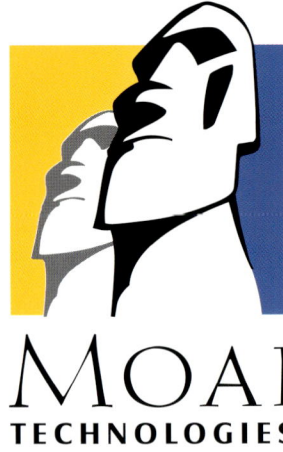

MOAI TECHNOLOGIES

6

STRATEGIC FOCUS CONSULTING

7

BridgeLinks
a systematic approach

8

1
BUSINESS LAYERS

2
WWW.BREAKAWAY.COM

3
COMPUTERGISTICS L.L.C.

4
SERVICE ADVISORS

5
COACH BERRY

6
MOAI TECHNOLOGIES

7
STRATEGIC FOCUS CONSULTING

8
BRIDGE LINKS

1
TRADE MATRIX YOUR COMPANY'S
B2B STRATEGY

2
COOL STRATEGIES

3
THOMSON TECHNOLOGY

4
LG TECHNICAL SOLUTIONS

5
KNOWLEDGE BASED SYSTEMS

6
TBM LEANSIGMA INSTITUTE

7
PARADIGM STRATEGY GROUP INC

8
MANAGEMENT OPTIONS

tradeMatrix™

Your Company $ B2B strategy

1

Knowledge Based Systems

5

cool *strategies*

2

TBM

6

THOMSON TECHNOLOGY

C O N S U L T I N G   G R O U P

3

Paradigm

7

LG Technical
Solutions

4

MANAGEMENT
OPTIONS

8

RedArrow
CONSULTING

1

zapthink

2

Technology Venture

3

JOHN SCHERER & ASSOCIATES
Transforming the world at work

4

FAMILY
LAW CENTER

5

CALICO®

6

CROSSROADS
Lagal Nurse Consultants

7

INTERNETWORK
expert

8

1
RED ARROW CONSULTING

2
ZAP THINK

3
TECHNOLOGY VENTURE ADVISORS,
LLC

4
JOHN SCHERER & ASSOCIATES

5
FAMILY LAW CENTER

6
CALICO EBUSINESS FOR LEADERS

7
CROSSROADS

8
INTERNET WORK EXPERT

management NEW LOGO

1
BERMAN MARKETING RESERVE

2
RESOLUTION ECONOMICS

3
G2 TEAM SALES

4
LAFFERTY

5
JAILBAIT

6
ECS CONSULTING ASSOCIATES

7
VITRIA

8
TECHNICALLY SPEAKING.LLC

1

resolution economics LLC

2

G2 TEAM SALES

3

LAFFERTY
KNOWLEDGE TO BANK ON

4

5

ECS
CONSULTING ASSOCIATES

6

VITRIA

7

8

103

ACNielsen

1

2

3

LEGAL SERVICESPLAN ®

4

IT Galaxy

5

6

7

8

Globe
ASSIST

9

1
ACNIELSEN

2
GRAND/ABACUS BUSINESS FORMS

3
SOVE

4
LEGAL SERVICESPLAN

5
IT GALAXY

6
KPMG CONSULTING

7
FORESIGHT CONSULTING INC

8
CVB CONSULTANTS

9
GLOBE ASSIST

1
BRAINCRAMPS

2
IT CONSUITING

3
PARKER LE PLA.BRAND DEVELO-
PMENT

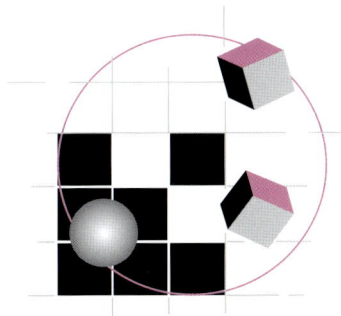

4
LIGHT HOUSE CONSULTING GROUP

5
CORAD O SOLUTIONS

6
U.S.A DVISOR

7
SYSTEMS CONSULTING GROUP.INC.

8
BIZIPA/CONSULTING FIRM

1

CORADO
S O L U T I O N S

5

IT Consuiting

2

U.S.A D V I S O R

TM

6

3

Systems Consulting Group, Inc.

7

LIGHT HOUSE
CONSULTING GROUP

4

BiZiPa

8

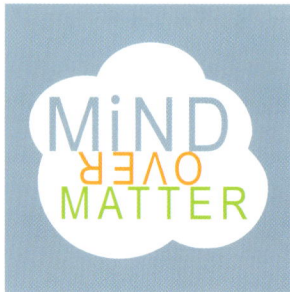

BUSINESS CUSTOMER MARKETING

1

1
BUSINESS CUSTOMER MARKETING

2
IN & OUTS

3
MIND OVER MATTER

4
RVM CONSULTING

5
MCMICHAEL AUMAN CONSULTANTS

6
CULINARY INNOVATION CONSUL-
TING & TRADING

7
TULSHI ICT SOLUTIONS LTD.

8
ALL BUSINESS

5

IN
&
OUTS

2

MiND
OVER
MATTER

3

Culinary
Innovation
consulting & trading

6

Tulshi
ICT Solutions Ltd

7

4

all.Business™
WE ARE SERIOUS ABOUT SERVICE

8

1
GRAEBE.DANNA & ASSOCIATES

2
SYNERGISTIC DEVELOPMENT.INC

3
CPI BUSINESS GROUPS

4
NET QUOTIENT CONSULTING GROUP

5
E-POWER

6
PREMENOS

7
HOME GAIN

8
STEAL STRATEGIES

GRAEBE, DANNA & ASSOCIATES
THE RIGHT PATH FOR
YOUR FINANCIAL FUTURE

1

e-power

5

Synergistic Development, Inc.
Trumbull, CT

2

Premenos®

6

CPI

BUSINESS GROUPS

3

HomeGain℠

7

Net Quotient
CONSULTING GROUP

4

STRATEGIES

8

107

IDC

1

grow

5

2

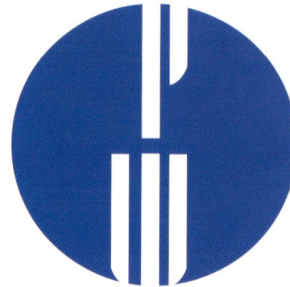

6

M

3

CAP GEMINI

7

BearingPoint™

4

8

1
IDC

2
TRANS SOLUTIONS

3
MW

4
BEARING POINT

5
GROW

6
PRICE WATERHOUSE

7
CAP GEMINI

8
BARRINGTON

1
CMG

2
LANGTON CHERUBINO

3
COMPLIANCE INC.

4
SWIFTOUCH

5
PUBLICIS CONSULTANTS

6
DIGITAL INSIGHT

7
EDGE WING

8
INFORMATION HIGHWAY.INC.

CMG

1

M S & L

5

2

DIGITAL INSIGHT

6

Compliance Inc.

3

EdgeWing

7

Swiftouch

4

INFORMATION HIGHWAY, INC.

8

1

2

3

4

5

6

7

1
QUALIFY

2
MAP INFO

3
FOR YOU 2 KNOW

4
SYNNEX

5
LEXIS NEXIS

6
KEYNOTE

7
«BUSINESS 2.0» JOB FAIR «business 2.0»

1
INFO WORLD TESTCENTER INSIGHT

2
RAINING DATA

3
INFO WORKS

4
MERCURY MESSENGER

5
CONCEPT INFORMATION SYSTEMS

6
IMR

7
INFO STAR

InfoWorld
TESTCENTER
INSIGHT

1

4

RainingData®

2

Concept
INFORMATION SYSTEMS

5

info
WORKS

3

IMR™

6

INFO STAR
INCORPORATED

7

111

TALENTKEEPERS™

1

Olsten
Staffing Services^{SM}

2

Bellingham Benefits
connecting active people
LLC

5

THE CAREER AGENT

3

KAISER RESOURCES INC.

6

RED HERRING
Job Pool

4

McIntosh
staffing resources

7

1
TALENT KEEPERS

2
OLSTEN STAFFING SERVICES

3
THE CAREER AGENT

4
RED HERRING JOB POOL

5
BELLINGHAM BENEFITS LLC

6
KAISER RESOURCES INC

7
MCINTOSH STAFFING RESOURCES

1
MUTUAL EMPLOYMENT.INC.

2
IT RADAR.COM

3
ELLIS PAGE ASSOCIATES

4
JOB SMACK

5
HEADHUNTER.COM

6
PEOPLE I KNOW

7
HARTE-HANKS.INC

8
SEARCBING RED

1

ITradar**.com**®

The eMarket for IT services℠

2

Ellis Page
Associates

3

4

5

iii
P E O P L E **i** K N O W

6

HARTE
HANKS

Harte-Hanks, Inc.

7

searchingRed.

8

KAISER PERMANENTE

1

BRENDLER ASSOCIATES, Inc.

2

Seek
Model and Talent Search

3

Smith Corona

4

5

6

ON THE
JOB
@
SCHWAB

7

1
KAISER PERMANENTE

2
BRENDLER ASSOCIATES.INC

3
SEEK MODEL AND TALENT SEARCH

4
SMITH CORONA

5
STAR ADVISORS

6
STAR ADVISORS

7
MARJORIE GROSS & CO INC

1
CYPRESS BEND

2
VUEPOINT.INC

3
ATM

4
SAFECO

5
ARDCO.INC.

6
EPIC INTERNATIONAL

7
ARGYLE ASSOCIATES

8
CLIVIA

CYPRESS BEND

1

Ardco

5

epic international

6

2

3

Argyle Associates

7

SAFECO

4

CLIVIA

8

eResources

1

The VanAllen Group, Inc.

2

OMRON
Sensing tomorrow ™

3

ANDON
UNLIMITED

4

5

ISMS
LTD

6

7

Trekker™

8

1
E RESOURCES.LNC

2
THE VANALLEN GROUP.INC.

3
OMRON SENSING TOMORROW

4
WIZARDS OF THE COAST

5
KATO INDUSTRIES

6
ISMS

7
HANYANG CO..LTD

8
ROCKWELL INTERNATIONAL

1
MAS GLOBAL ENTERPRISES

2
AVEO.INC

3
SIMCO

4
WINTERBERSY LANE

5
AD

6
THE HILTON HEAD

7
VETRA

GLOBAL ENTERPRISES

MAS

1

4

AVEO

2

5

6

TRACHER

3

vetra

7

QualTech International

1

SeaChange CORPORATION

2

3

A R C

5

6

FantasticOne

4

Netigy ℠

7

1
QUAL TECH INTERNATIONAL

2
SEA CHANGE

3
DONGYANG CONFECTIONARY

4
FANTASTIC ONE

5
ARC INTERNATIONAL INC

6
BRONSON BROTHERS INC

7
NETIGY CORPORATION

1
BEECKEN PETTY & COMPANY

2
BACKYANG

3
COMMCOR INC

4
RIVER NORTH ASSOCIATION

5
OBAYASHI CORPORATION

6
COEX

7
COMMAX

8
RECONDA INTERNATIONAL CORP-
ORATION

9
ALLAN COX & ASSOCIATES

10
VIACARE.INC

3

7

4

8

1

5

9

2

6

10

119

新邦

1

FABERGÉ
POWER
STICK®

2

The Adler Group Inc.

3

4

MEDICUS GROUP INTERNATIONAL

M GROUP

5

continuum

6

conversus group

7

KIMPTON GROUP™

8

1
SHINBANG CO.LTO

2
FABERGE

3
THE ADLER GROUP.INC

4
ESSPIA

5
MEDICUS GROUP INTERNATIONA

6
CONTINUUM

7
CONVERSUS GROUP

8
KIMPTON HOTEL GROUP

1
ONE FAIR OAKS

2
BIRM

3
SUN COKE COMPANY

4
GAUNTLETT GROUP

5
ACTIVERSE

6
MAGNA-CHECK CORPORATION

7
FINE CORPORATION

ONE
FAIR
OAKS

1

4

Activerse™

5

2

6

3

FINE Corporation

7

121

MERRITT

1

BECKLEY IMPORTS

2

3

MENLO WORLDWIDE

4

5

6

KANGAROO

7

SPARK HOLDINGS

8

1
MERRITT

2
BECKLEY IMPORTS

3
UCHINO

4
MENLO WORLD WIDE

5
THE MERIT SYSTEM

6
SIGNATURE GROUP

7
KANGAROO

8
SPARK HOLDINGS

1
TUMI INCORPORATED

2
TANDEM

3
OMINIDIA.INC

4
HYUNDAI

5
NIEHAUS RYAN GROUP

6
KYUKEN CO..LTD

7
HILLHAVEN CORPORATION

8
CARLETON CORPORATION

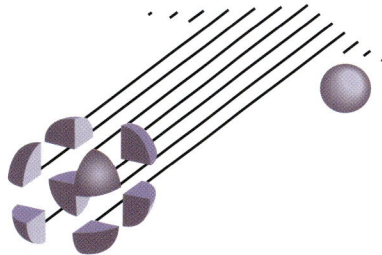

1

5

2

6

3

7

4

8

The *Ditka* Corporation

1

MITOKOR
THE MITOCHONDRIA COMPANY

2

FIELD OF DREAMS
enterprises

3

TIGERS®
SUCCESS SERIES

4

BAIGLOBAL

5

6

7

OpenCon Systems, Inc.
WORLDWIDE COMMUNICATIONS SOLUTIONS

8

1
THE DITKA CORPORATION

2
MITO KOR INC

3
"FIELD OF DREAMS" ENTERPR-
ISES

4
TIGERS SUCCESS SERIES

5
BAI GLOBAL

6
HEINZ

7
CREST INTERNATIONAL

8
OPENCON SYSTEMS INC

1
ASTARIS

2
DOOSAN INDUSTRIES

3
QUALITEK

4
ITT INDUSTRIES

5
LOM INDUSTRIES

6
BATTERY CORP

7
PRIDCO PUERTO RICO INDUSTR-
IAL DEVELOPMENT COMPANY

8
HIGHLAND FEATHER

ASTARIS™
Quality Products. Exceptional Response.

1

5

DOOSAN

2

BatteryCorp

6

QUALITEK

3

PRIDCO

7

ITT Industries
Engineered for life

4

Highland Feather

8

COMPACT TECHNOLOGY

1

experient™

5

Centilium Technology

2

K

6

3

GERBER

7

scitex

4

GCSS ARMY
Global Combat Support System-Army

8

1
COMPACT TECHNOLOGY

2
CENTILIUM TECHNOLOGY

3
TECHCOM PARTNERS

4
SCITEX CORPORATION.LTD

5
EXPERIENT

6
KAZ TECHNOLOGIES

7
GERBER

8
GCSS ARMY

1
MICELL TECHNOLOGIES INC.

2
GORE

3
ZAIQ TECHNOLOGIES INC.

4
PLX TECHNOLOGY

5
RECOURSE TECHNOLOGIES

6
ERGOCENTRICS

7
DULLES TECH CENTER

PLX
TECHNOLOGY
4

Hangers™
1

Recourse
Technologies
5

GORE
*Creative Technologies
Worldwide*
2

6

Z A i Q
3

DULLES TECH CENTER
7

uberLAN
TECHNOLOGIES

1

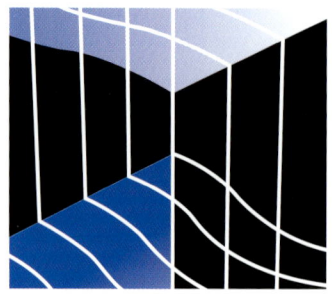

Health
Science
Solutions

2

UJAMAA
TECHNICAL SUPPORT
& COMPUTER SERVICES

3

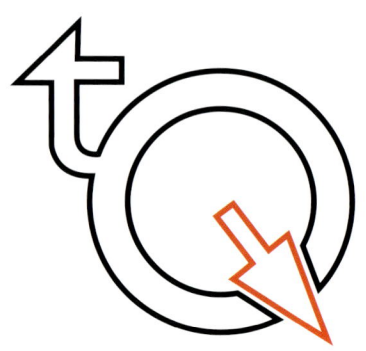

4

PEAK
TECHNOLOGIES
CORPORATION

5

6

7

aspire

IVY Technologies™

8

1
UBER LAN

2
HEALTH SCIENCE SOLUTIONS

3
UJAMAA TECHNICAL SUPPORT &
COMPUTER SERVICES

4
TECH QUARTER

5
PEAK

6
ALTEC LANSING TECHNOLOGIES

7
ASPIRE TECHNOLOGY GROUP

8
IVY TECBNOLOGIES

1
SEQUOIA TECHNOLOGY

2
OPINN SKOGUR

3
BLACK STONE

4
EXE TECHNOLOGIES

5
ANERGEN INC

6
ADTECH

7
CORDANT TECHNOLOGIES

8
EICON TECHNOLOGY

SEQUOIA
TECHNOLOGY

1

Anergen

5

OPINN SKÓGUR

2

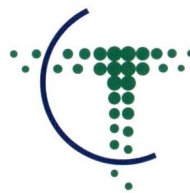

ADTECH™

6

BLACKSTONE

3

Cordant
Technologies™

Howmet · Huck · Thiokol

7

EXE TECHNOLOGIES

4

EICON
TECHNOLOGY

8

129

X Technology

1

2

BIOTECH
CONNECTION

You, Monsanto and the World

3

B E N E V I A

4

THUMB
SCRIPT

5

6

MERCURY INTERACTIVE

7

1
X TECHNOLOGY

2
ORIS TECHNOLOGIES

3
MONSANTO COMPANY

4
BENEVIA MONSANTO CORPORATION

5
THUMB SCRIPT

6
STARDUST TECHNOLOGIES INC

7
MERCURY INTERACTIVE

1
NANOCOSM TECHNOLOGIES

2
RENAUDFOSTER

3
OKPX TECHNOLOGIES

4
MARKET SCIENCES

5
SYNAPT TECHNOLOGIES

6
ELECTRONIC BOOK TECHNOLOGIES.
INC

7
SCIMAT SCIENTIFIC MACHINERY.
INC

8
TECHNOLOGY CHAMBERS

1

Synapt
T E C H N O L O G I E S

5

RENAUDFOSTER

2

ebt

6

kpx
TECHNOLOGIES

3

SCIMAT

7

MARKET
SCIENCES

4

8

BREECE

1

Invitrogen™

2

VISTA

CONTROL SYSTEMS

3

6

TRADEX

TECHNOLOGIES

5

United Technologies

4

ADVANTAGE

8

1
BREECE

2
INVITROGEN

3
VISTA CONTROL SYSTEMS

4
UNITED TECHNOLOGIES

5
TRADEX TECHNOLOGIES

6
DIAMMOND TECHNOLOGY PARTNERS

7
CENTURION TECHNOLOGIES

8
ADVANTAGE TECHNOLOGIES

7

1
GUI DANCE TEHNOLOGIES INC

2
PRIMETECH

3
ROBERT HALF TECHNOLOGY

4
SYMBOL

5
PREFERENCE THCHNOLOGIES

6
AZTEC TECHNOLOQY PARTENERS.
INC.

7
RENO TECHNOLOGY

symbol ®

4

1

PREFERENCE TECHNOLOGIES

5

PRIMETECH

2

AZTEC TECHNOLOQY PARTENERS, INC.

6

RH
ROBERT HALF
TECHNOLOGY ®

3

RENO
►**TECHNOLOGY**◄

7

133

1
GAZELLE TECHNOLOGIES

2
MUSE TECHNOLOGICS

3
RED FISH TECHNOLOGY

4
AMERSHAM BIOSCIENCES

5
PEGA

6
JAVELIN TECHNOLOGIES

7
FORTRESS TECHNOLOGIES.LNC.

8
GPG TECHNOLOGIES

1

Pega

5

2

JAVELIN TECHNOLOGIES

6

REDFISH
TECHNOLOGY

3

FORTRESS **IM**

7

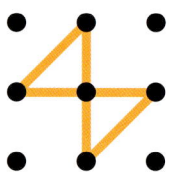
Amersham
Biosciences

4

FreshSeal™

8

1
GEORGIA TECH HOTEL AND CON-
FERENCE CENTER

2
AIR QUALITY LABORATORY

3
FOOD SERVICES OF AMERICA I-
NSTITUTION

4
GREAT LAKES SCIENCE CENTER

5
TRANSFORMING OUR ENERGY

6
DIABETES RESEARCH INSTITUTE

7
BARLOW RESEARCH ASSOCIATES
INC

Georgia Tech **Hotel and Conference Center**

1

Air Quality Laboratory

2

T R A N S F O R M I N G O U R E N E R G Y

5

3

6

4

BARLOW RESEARCH ASSOCIATES, INC.

7

1

2

sheffield haworth

3

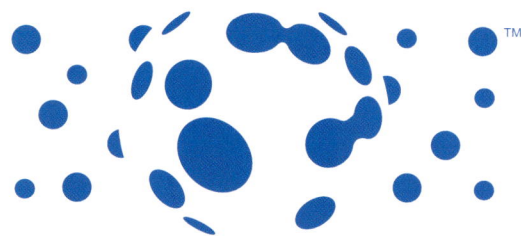

SETI INSTITUTE

4

5

The Kinsey Institute For Research
in Sex, Gender and Reproduction

6

7

7

1
GROUP HARMONY

2
UTILITIES PROTECTION CENTER

3
SHEFFIELD HAWORTH

4
SETI INSTITUTE

5
THE VEIN CENTER

6
THE KINSEY INSTITUTE

7
WEBER

8
ANTISOMA

1
NEO MEDIA TECHNOLOGIES

2
AMR

3
LEAPFROG MARKETING RESEARCH

4
INFORMATION TECHNOLOGY TRAIN-
ING ASSOCIATION

5
AQUA RESEARCH

6
GENETICS/HUMAN GENOME

7
VITEC MULTIMEDIA

1

Information Technology Training Association

4

A D V A N C E D
MANUFACTURING
R E S E A R C H

2

AQUARESEARCH

5

6

Leapfrog

Marketing Research

3

PRODUCTS

VITEC MULTIMEDIA

TECHNOLOGY

7

1
TECHNOLOGY SOURCE

2
CENTER FOR POPULATION HEA-
LTH AND NUTRITION

3
INSTITUTE FOR HEALTHY AGING

4
CENTER FOR SPEECH & LANGUAGE
DISORDERS

5
AMERICAN INSTITUTE OF WINE
& FOOD

6
KANSAS HEALTH FOUNDATION /L-
EADERSHIP SEMINAR

7
TARA LABS

8
ADVANCED LASER GRAPHICS

1

2

5

6

INSTITUTE FOR
HEALTHY
AGING

3

7

4

ADVANCED LASER
GRAPHICS

8

1
INTERNATIONAL FOOD POLICY
RESEARCH INSTITUTE

2
AURA-ASSOCIATION OF UNIVER-
SITIES FOR RESEARCH IN AST-
RONOMY INC

3
NATIONAL POLICY AND RESOURCE
CENTER ON WOMEN & AGING

4
RISS/RESEARC INSTITUTE FOR
SOCIAL SAFETY

5
INVESTOR IQ.COM

6
UNIVERSITY OF MIAMI ROSENST-
IEL SCHOOL OF MARINE AND AT-
MOSPHERIC SCIENCE

7
THE MARINE MAMMAL CENTER

IFPRI

1

RISS

4

investoriQ.com

5

AURA

2

investoriQ.com

NATIONAL POLICY AND
RESOURCE CENTER ON
WOMEN & AGING

3

The
Marine Mammal
Center

7

VERTURE ARCHITECTS

1

BANEI

4

GARDEN
ARCHITECTURE

5

3

GSD&M

6

Carlson West Povondra **Architects**

7

1
VERTURE ARCHITECTS

2
HOK ARCHITECTS

3
KOREA CONSTRUCTION MANAGEMENT
CORPORATION

4
BANEI SANGYO

5
GARDEN ARCHITECTURE

6
GSD & M

7
CARLSON WEST POVONDRA ARCHI-
TECTS

1
NATIONAL ASSOCIATION OF HOME
BUILDERS

2
RAFN

3
MARSON CONSTRUCTIONS

4
INSITE ARCHITECTURE

5
HOLLIN FRANKFURT

6
MILLER–NORRIS

7
LINDA & MANUEL HERRERA

1

INSITE
ARCHITECTURE

4

2

MARSON
CONSTRUCTIONS

3

1

4

1
PAN AMERICAN WORLD CONGRESS
OF ARCHITECTS

2
COMPLEX

3
BURR BARQUET ARCHITECTS

4
THE JERDE PARTNERSHIP

5
BREDAR WAGGONER ARCHITECTURE

6
ATTICUS SCRIBE

COMPLEX

2

5

ATTICUS

SCRIBE

6

BURR
BARQUET
architects

3

1
MONETA GROUP INC

2
MINKO CONSTRUCTION CO.

3
CHUNGGOO CONSTRUCTION

4
WILLIAMS CONSTRUCTION

5
TEAYOUNG CONSTRUCTION

6
PYRAMID CONSTRUCTIONS

7
HOUSE HOLDER

1

5

2

Pyramid

6

3

4

HOUSEHOLDER

7

1
READING ENTERTAINMENT

2
GARAGE OUTFITTERS INC

3
KYOWA AGENT CO LTD

4
ONSITE CONSTRUCTION

5
PROTEA TECHNOLOGIES

6
HOOPEN GARDNER CONSTRUCTION CO

7
HUMBER CONSTRUCTION

8
NEW SOUTH CONSTRUCTION

1

5

Garage Outfitters INC

2

HOOPENGARDNER CONSTRUCTION CO. SINCE 1981

6

KYOWA

3

HUBER CONSTRUCTION

7

ONSITE *Construction*

4

NEW SOUTH

8

1
RYOWA LIFE CREATE

2
SEOHO CONSTRUCTION

3
WILLIAMS CONSTRUCTION

4
ALEXANDER CONSTRUCTION.INC

5
TAKAGI KOMUTEN CO.LTD

6
CHRISTY CONSTRUCTION

7
ASTOR CONSTRUCTION

8
HASEBE KENSETSU CO.LTD

RYOWA
LIFE CREATE

1

TAKAGI

5

2

6

Williams Construction

3

7

ALEXANDER
CONSTRUCTION INC.

4

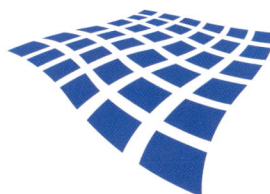

8

**PLAZA
BUILDERS
INC.**

1

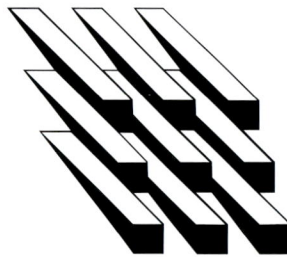

**Real Estate
Energy Solutions**

2

SM

**SWEET
CONSTRUCTION
CORPORATION**

3

BOULLIOUN

6

MACDONALD CONSTRUCTION

7

5

4

8

1
PLAZA BUILDERS INC

2
REAL ESTATE ENERGY SOLUTIONS

3
SWEET CONSTRUCTION CORPORAT-
ION

4
Minkoff CORPORATION

5
PASLODE

6
BOULLIOUN

7
MACDONALD CONSTRUCTION

8
EFCO CORPORATION

1
CREAG CONSTRUCTION

2
DRAKE DUNN

3
HARDIN CONSTRUCTION

4
EPI GENERAL CONTRACTORS

5
CONCO CONSTRUCTION

6
EDJE BOARDS

7
MDB CONTRACTING LLC

CREAG

1

CONCO
CONSTRUCTION

5

DRAKE
DUNN

2

EDJE

6

General
Contractors

4

HARDIN

3

MDB
CONTRACTING • LLC

7

1

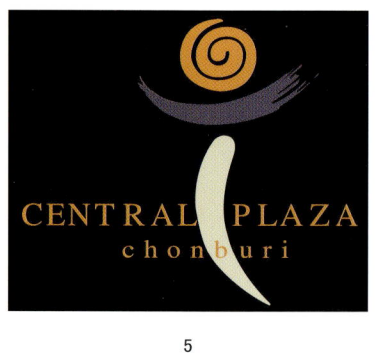

CENTRAL PLAZA
chonburi

5

1
CORPOREX CENTER

2
HASKELL CORPORATION

3
INFOPLAZA

4
MOSCOW BUSINESS CENTER

5
CENTRAL PLAZA

6
THE EQUITABLE BUILDING

7
WORLDWIDE PLAZA

6iXTH
STREET
WATERFRONT
PROPERTIES

2

THE EQUITABLE BUILDING

6

infoplaza

3

Moscow Business Center

4

WORLDWIDE
PLAZA

7

1
CONRAD INTERNATIONAL PLAZA

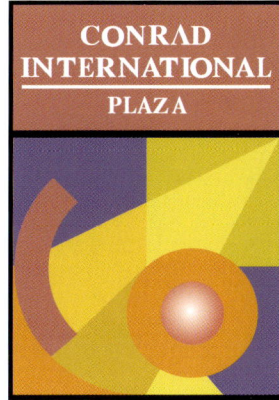

2
BARCLAY TOWERS

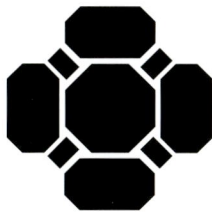

3
SPRING CREEK TOWERS

4
POWELL GARDENS

5
ROBERT SHARP TOM BOURDEAUX

6
CAPITOL TOWER

7
ESPLANADE PLACE

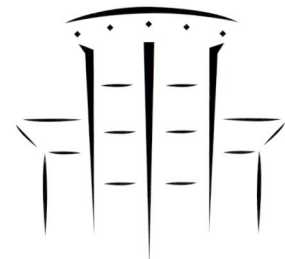

CONRAD INTERNATIONAL PLAZA

1

P O W E L L
G A R D E N S

4

BARCLAY TOWERS

2

M

5

CAPITOLTOWER

6

SPRING CREEK
Towers

3

ESPLANADE
Place

7

149

1

CorVu

Your Window Into The Future

5

1
FLEISCHMANN OFFICE INTERIORS

2
GUTTER HELMET

3
INCLINATOR COMPANY OF AME-
RICA

4
DOUBLEGREEN LANDSCAPES

5
CORVU

6
HOUSE DOCTOR HANDYMAN SERVI-
CES

7
COMMAND-AIR PTE LTD

GutterHelmet®
GUTTER PROTECTION SYSTEMS

2

HOME REPAIRS

HOUSE DOCTORS®
HANDYMAN SERVICE

6

INCLINATOR
COMPANY OF AMERICA

3

4

7

1
BEACH HOUSE RENTALS OF DEST-
IN,LLC

2
SERRANO INTERIORS

3
PATRICIA ABAD INTERIOR DESI-
GNER

4
MIRKO HOCEVAR, LJUBIJANA

5
DRIP DOCTORS

1

2

4

3

5

miro

1

La Strada

2

ravel

3

1
MIRO HOUSING DEVELOPMENT

2
LA STRADA HOUSING DEVELOPMENT

3
RAVEL HOUSING DEVELOPMENT

1
MID—MICHIGAN MASONRY

2
TEAM EMERGENT

3
FIRST UNION COMMUNITY REINV—
ESTMENT

4
OVERBERG DREAM TEAM

5
RAINTREE HOMES

6
E.SPEER&ASSOCIATES

7
CHANGE OF PLACE REALTY

MidMichigan Masonry
COMMERCIAL MASONS

1

DREAM
Overberg Team

4

Team
Emergent

2

5

3

Change
of Place
REALTY

6

7

Samuel-Lawrence
Real Estate Services, LLC

1

2

3

Ridere

4

RCDC

5

RANCHO DOS CAÑADAS

6

PROPERTY GROUP

7

1
SAMUEL-LAWRENCE REAL ESTATE S-
ERVICES, LLC

2
DANCING BEAR ESTATES

3
CENTRAL

4
RIDERE

5
RCDC

6
RANCHO DOS CANADAS

7
PROPERTY GROUP

1
BAXLEY DEVELOPMENT.INC

2
BRIDLE WOOD

3
BENTLEY PROPERTIES

4
CHANGING PLACES. LLC

5
MONEY 4 YOUR HOME

6
JDC HOMES.LLC

7
PETTIFER & ASSOCIATES

Baxley
development, inc.

1

5

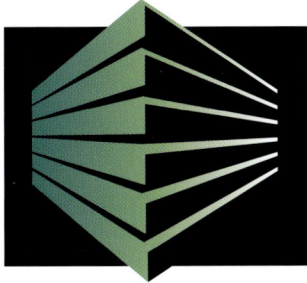

BRIDLEWOOD

2

BENTLEY

PROPERTIES

3

jdc
HOMES, LLC

6

Changing
Places, LLC

4

Pettifer & Associates
REAL ESTATE VALUATION EXPERTS

7

Home State Buyes

REAL ESTATE

5

1
CONTINENTAL DEVELOPMENT GRO-
UP.INC

2
LIFECARE SANTAFE

3
MCKEE NELSON

4
SL GREEN REALTY CORP

5
HOME STATE BUYES

6
BEDFORD PROPERTIES

7
INTERBAY HOMES

1

LIFECARE

SANTA FE

2

McKee Nelson

3

6

SL GREEN
REALTY CORP.

4

ib

INTERBAY
HOMES

7

1
RENT TECH

2
RUTENBERG HOMES

3
O'KANE REALTY

4
KCG

5
DONGSIN HOUSING

6
HARR FAMILY HOMES—SEDONA

7
TEMPO MECHANICAL

Rent Tech

1

Rutenberg Homes

2

5

O'KANE REALTY

3

SEDONA

6

KCG REALTY

4

Tempo

7

casamia

1

2

3

4

MOUNTAIN
trading co.

5

6

Urban Village
REALTORS INC.

7

1
CASAMIA

2
HOUSE WORKS HOME LLC

3
LENNOX

4
MOUNTAIN TRADING CO.

5
BRAD BACHMAN HOMES INC

6
BIG GREEN PLANTS/LEE CASEY

7
URBAN VILLAGE REALTORS INC

1
MCDONALD DEVELOPMENT COMPANY

2
LOWE DEVELOPMENT CORPORATION

3
RELO

4
MANES SPACE

5
QUOTES & NOTES

6
CONDO EXCHANGE

7
THE HARBORSIDE CORPRATION

1

5

2

6

LEADING
REAL ESTATE
COMPANIES
OF THE WORLD

3

7

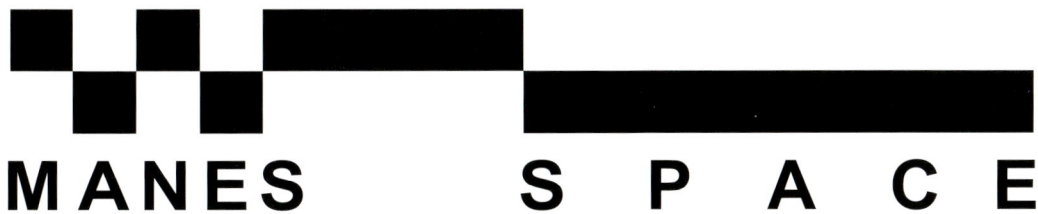

MANES SPACE

4

HomeWorks™

RACTO
YAMASHINA

meadowlark

Chain
Development
創建發展公司

TURNING POINT
realty advisors, LLC

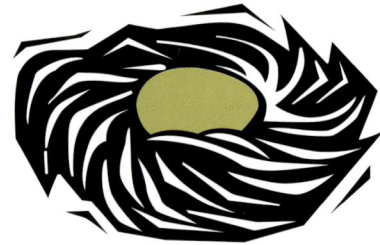

The
LEGACY
Group, Inc.

1
HOME WORKS

2
YAMASHINA EKIMAE REDEVELOPM-
ENT

3
MEADOWLARK

4
CHAIN DEVELOPMENT

5
TURNING POINT

6
ADDISON HOMES

7
THE LEGACY GROUP,INC

1
DEAN WITTER REALTY

2
HANLEY WOOD INC

3
CDA

4
REYNOLDS CUSTOM HOMES

5
SUMMIT REAL ESTATE

6
A VISION OF THE FUTURE

7
MAUNA KEA REALTY

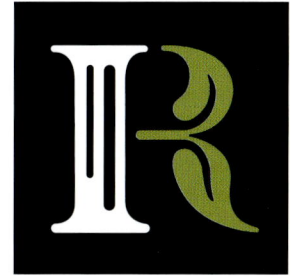

4

1

2

SUMMIT
REAL ESTATE

5

A VISION OF THE FUTURE

6

CDA

Copper Development Association

3

MAUNA KEA REALTY

7

Gazelle

1

2

3

4

1
GAZELLE

2
MOUNTAIN TRADING CO.

3
KOREA LAND DEVELOPMENT CORP

4
SOUTHERN OREGON APPRAISAL S-
ERVICES

5
FISHER

6
NEST INC

7
TAYLOR & MATHIS

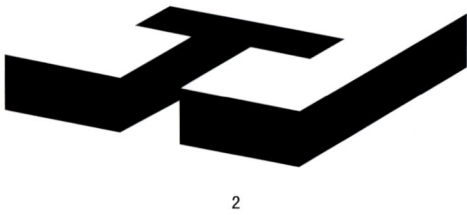

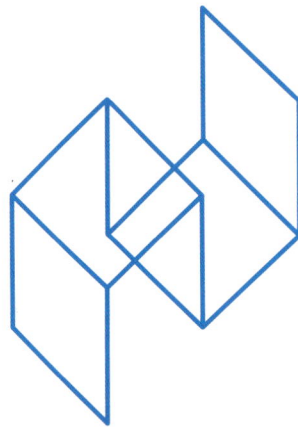

5

real estate dealer & agency

NEST,INC.

6

7

1
WESTERN DEVELOPMENT CORP

2
TEUBNER

3
STANDARD PACIFIC

4
BETZ DEARBORN

5
EXITOGAR

6
REGENT PROPERTIES

7
KALBERER

FRANKLIN MILLS

1

EXITOGAR

5

TEUBNER
& ASSOCIATES, INC.

2

REGENT PROPERTIES

6

STANDARD PACIFIC

3

4

7

KEEPING LAWNS HEALTHY FOR LIFE®

1

APARTMENTMANAGER

2

HARTMAN'S
LANDSCAPE & MAINTENANCE

4

CUSHMAN &
WAKEFIELD R

5

MACK-CALI™

6

1
LAWN DOCTOR

2
APARTMENT MANAGER

3
CORPORATE PROPERTY CONSULT-
ANTS

4
HARTMAN'S LANDSCAPE & MAIN-
TENANCE

5
CUSHMAN & WAKEFIELD

6
MACK-CALI

1
INTEGRA

2
DRAKE PROPERTY GROUP

3
LLOYD YOUNGERLTD LANDSCAPE MAN-
AGEMENT SERVICES.

4
ASHLAND MAINTENANCE

5
BEDFORD PROPERTIES

6
PROCUREMENT & LOGISTICS

7
FOTH & VAN DYKE-STRATEGIC E-
NVIRONMENTAL MANAGEMENT

Integra
Property Services, LLc

1

2

SINCE 1935

ASHLAND MAINTENANCE

4

5

Procurement & Logistics

6

LLOYD
YOUNGER LTD
landscape management services

3

**Strategic
Environmental
Management**

7

CNF
TRANSPORTATION

1

1
CNF TRANSPORTATION

2
TAXI SERVICE

3
BRAVO.BUS

4
CHARLOTTE MOTOR SPEEDWAY

5
TRIPLE A BARRICADE

6
KEY CITY TRANSPORT INC

4

TAXI SERVICE

2

5

B R A V O · B U S

3

6

1
TAKATORI LOGISTICS CORPORA-
TION

2
21 CENTURY LOGISFICS

3
PORT AUTHORITY OF NY & NJ

4
PROT OF PITTSBURGH

5
PITTSBURGH LIGNT RAIL
TRANSIT SYSTEM

6
RYDER

7
SEOUL METROPOLITAN RAPID
TRANSIT CORPORATION

Takatori
Logistics Corporation

1

4

2

5

6

3

7

Transtar

1

all settled group
delivering fair market value

2

Planet Cargo
The smartest move on the planet

3

TransporTec

5

6

INNOLOG™
The Future of Supply Chain Logistics

7

4

1
TRANSTAR.INC

2
ALL SETTLED GROUP

3
PLANET CARGO

4
TEXAS DEPARTMENT OF TRANSPO-
RTATION

5
EAST JAPAN TRANSPORT TECHNO-
LOGY

6
TUCSON

7
INNOLOG

1
THE CENTRAL EXCHANGE

2
OWENS & MINOR

3
XELUS

4
HUB GROUP.INC.

5
SKY TEAM

6
COFIROUTE-THE EXPRESS
HIGHWAY

7
EAST COAST TRANSPORTATION
SYSTEMS INC.

T H E
CENTRAL EXCHANGE

1

Hub Group, Inc.

4

S K Y T E A M

5

OM

2

COFIROUTE

6

X E L U S

3

East Coast Transportation Systems inc.

7

BRITISH AIRWAYS

1

*air*Jamaica

2

QANTAS

3

AVBASE
A V I A T I O N

6

Cessna
A Textron Company

4

O R I E N T

A I R L I N E S

A S S O C I A T I O N

7

NORTHWEST
A I R L I N E S
Connect**First**℠

5

1
BRITISH AIRWAYS

2
AIR JAMAICA

3
QANTAS

4
CESSNA

5
NORTHWEST AIRLINES

6
AVBASE AVIATION

7
ORIENT AIRLINES ASSOCIATION

1
AERO MEXICO

2
AIR NEW ZEALAND

3
LOS ANGELES WORLD AIRPORTS

4
E BUSINESS CONFERENCE AND
EXPO

5
ASIANA AIRLINES

6
AIRBUS

7
MALAYSIA AIRLINES

8
CONTINENTAL

1

5

2

6

3

7

4

8

171

Air Equine

1

VANGUARD AIRLINES

2

1
AIR EQUINE

2
VANGUARD AIRLINES

3
NORTHWEST AIRLINES

4
PHILIPPINE AIRLINES

5
CORP AIR

6
SKY RISE

7
MC CAULEY PROPELLERS

8
CS CREATIVE/AMERICAN AIRLINES

5

SKYRISE

6

50 YEARS

BRIDGING the PACIFIC

3

McCAULEY™

7

Philippine Airlines

4

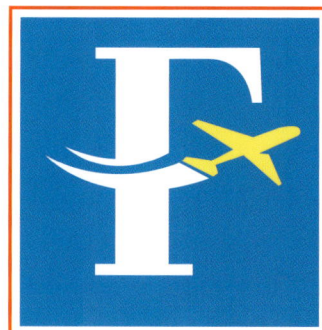

8

CARIBBEAN

AQUASTAR

1

2

WORLD'S LEADING
CRUISE LINES

3

ORIENT LINES®
THE DESTINATION CRUISE SPECIALISTS

4

5

HELM
CORPORATION

6

THE WEST INDIAN COMPANY LIMITED
WICO

7

1
MONSANTO

2
CLIPPER CRUISE LINE

3
WORLD'S LEADING CRUISE LINES

4
ORIENT LINES

5
DENRAY TIRE

6
HELM CORPORATION

7
THE WEST INDIAN COMPANY.LTD.

1
SEATRAIN LINES

2
CRUISE WEST

3
CRUISE ONE

4
BASTION SHIPPING

5
SUMEREST HOUSEBOATS

6
MISS CIRCLE LINE

7
SONESTA HOTELS.RESORTS & NI-
LE CRUSES

8
SEAPORT LIBERTY CRUISES

1

5

2

CRUISEONE.

3

6

Sonesta Hotels, Resorts
& Nile Cruises

7

4

8

1
KUROGU

2
ROYAL CARIBBEAN INTERNATIONAL

3
FINCANTIERI CRUISE SHIPS

4
WINDSTAR CRUISES

5
YACHTSMANS EXCHANGE

6
HAKATA BAY MARINA CRUISE

7
PACHAMAMA'S NEW WORLD CUISINE

1

5

RoyalCaribbean
INTERNATIONAL ®

2

FINCANTIERI

3

6

WINDSTAR®
C R U I S E S

4

PACHAMAMA'S
NEW WORLD CUISINE

7

Lucunt Technologie

acela®

MOBILEQ™

OnStar®

everypath

THE BIG GIANT PHONE COMPANY

JABRA®

Lightwave Communications, Inc.

1
ACELA

2
ON STAR

3
THE BIG GIANT PHONE COMPANY

4
LIGHTWAVE COMMUNICATIONS.INC.

5
MOBILEQ

6
EVERY PATH

7
JABRA

1

5

2

6

3

7

4

1
NTT DO CO MO

2
PORTICO ON THE GO

3
NEXTEL

4
ERICSSON

5
MOTIENT

6
HOME LINK WIRELESS CONTROL S-
YSTEM

7
TELLA

8
VERIZON

1

2

HomeLink®
Wireless Control System

6

nextel.
WIRELESS·NETWORK

3

TELIA

7

ERICSSON

4

verizon

8

GDS 2.0

1

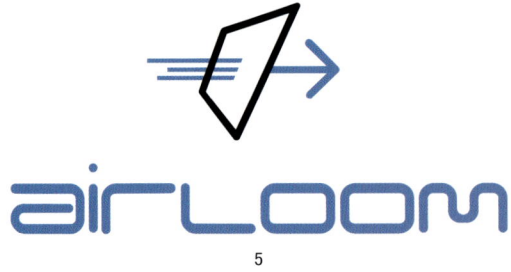

POLYCOM®
Advanced Teleconferencing Solutions

2

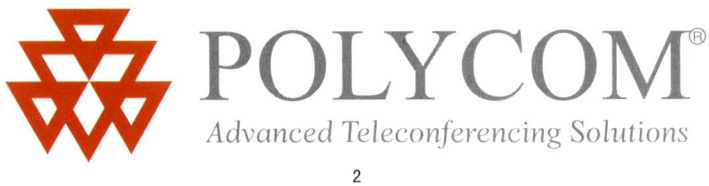

fastpoint

3

airloom

5

1
GLOBAL DIAL SERVICES

2
POLYCOM

3
FASTPOINT

4
SUMMIT COMMUNICATION SERVIC-
ES,INC.

5
AIRLOOM

6
OUT DIAL SYSTEMS

7
REQV

Outdial
SYSTEMS

6

eQrV
videoconferencing

reliability . ease of use . quality . value

7

SUMMIT COMMUNICATION SERVICES, INC.

4

1
SING TEL

2
MOSTEL

3
LGC WIRELESS

4
NUANCE

5
ORASCOM TEIECOM

6
ROAD RUNNER

7
ERRANDS UNLIMITED

8
WAVE WIRELESS NETWORKING

SingTel

1

ORASCOM
TELECOM

5

2

ROAD RUNNER

6

LGC WIRELESS

3

7

nuance
communications

4

w⌀ve ™
WIRELESS NETWORKING

8

181

wireless

1

Triple-E
Satellites

5

NightSoft

WIRELESS TECHNOLOGY

2

inPhonic

6

BT

3

T · · Mobile · ®

7

city wide
Communications

4

talk-a-lot
WIRELESS

8

1
WIRELESS SOLUTIONS

2
NIGHT SOFT WIRELESS TECHNOL-
OGY

3
BT

4
CITY WIDE COMMUNICATIONS

5
TRIPLE-E SATELLITES

6
IN PHONIC

7
T-MOBILE

8
TALK-A-LOT WIRELESS

1
OPASTCO

2
LIBAN CELL

3
GLOBAL ONE

4
THE GLOBALSERVE CORPORATION

5
AKARA

6
BROADWING

7
KCC INFROMATION & COMMUNICA-
TION

8
MCI

OPASTCO

1

AKARA

5

2

Broadwing

6

Global One SM

3

7

4

MCI

8

1

5

Telecellular, Inc.

2

wireless**knowledge**

6

Agilent Technologies

Innovating the HP Way

3

**Wireless
Financial
Services**

7

AT&T

4

AMERICAN
TELECOM
INCORPORATED

8

1
WEBTELECOM

2
TELE CELLULAR.INC

3
AGILENT TECHNOLOGIES

4
AT & T

5
COVIGO

6
WIRELESS KNOWLEDGE/QUALCOMM

7
WIRELESS FINANCIAL SERVICES

8
AMERICAN TELECOM INCORPORATED

1
MONSOON

2
MOBILITY

3
BLACK BERRY

4
FIRST WORLD COMMUNICATIONS

5
INFOLIO

6
INTELLI SPACE

7
ON SITE COMMUNICATION INC

8
SAME DAY SHIPPING

1

5

Mobility

2

6

3

On-Site

7

FirstWorld™
COMMUNICATIONS

4

8

1

2

3

unimobile™

4

OS OmniSky™

5

MOBILITAS

6

United States
Post Office

7

CONEXANT™

8

telexcel

9

1
U-CONNECT

2
PCCW

3
AIR 2 WEB

4
UNIMOBILE

5
OMNI SKY

6
MOBILITAS

7
UNITED STATES POST OFFICE

8
CONEXANT

9
TELEXCEL

1
WIRED POCKET

2
HONG KONG

3
DISH NETWORK

4
POST & TELECOMMUNICATIONS OF
FINLAND

5
OPTICAL CABLE CORPORATION

6
CINGULAR WIRELESS

7
BELL ATLANTIC

wired
pocket

1

4

2

OPTICAL CABLE
CORPORATION
www.occfiber.com

5

cingular SM
WIRELESS

6

dish
NETWORK

3

Bell Atlantic

7

1

MERC
DELIVERY

4

BoxItUp
Express Delivery

5

Z *zipcar* ®

2

exel

6

FROG EXPRENCE

3

Whippet
Despatch

7

1
COFFEIN DELIVERY

2
ZIPCAR

3
FROG EXPRESS

4
MERC DELIVERY

5
BOXIT UP EXPRESS DELIVERY

6
EXEL

7
WHIPPET DESPATCH

NATIONAL COMPAIGN FOR HEARING
HEALTH

1

CULVER CITY
UNIFIED SCHOOL DISTRICT

4

1
ART CENTER COLLEGE OF DESIGN
ALUMNI COUNCIL

2
HOOKED ON PHONICS

3
HARCOURT BRACE EDUCATIONAL
MEASUREMENT

4
CULVER CITY UNIFIED SCHOOL
DISTRICT

hooked on phonics

2

Metropolitan Achievement Test   Eighth Edition

3

1
SPEAKING OF PAIN

2
ALL-STARS CHEMISTRY AND BIO-
SCIENCE

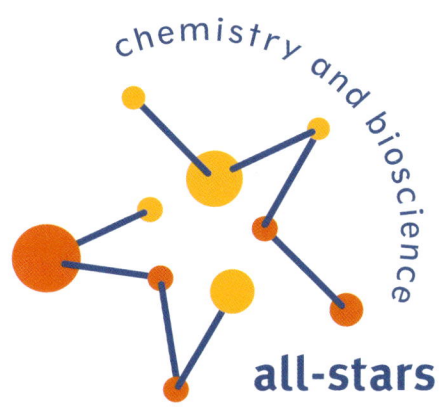

3
LINCOLN ELEMENTARY SCHOOL
PTA AILEEN OWENS

4
KYONGBUK UNIVERSITY OF FOR-
EIGN STUDIES

5
hooked on phonics

6
FAMILY CONNECTION

7
COMPREHENSIVE LANGUAGE SERVICES

SPEAKING OF PAIN

1

KUFS

4

HOP™

5

chemistry and bioscience
all-stars

2

6

JOURNEYS

3

7

1

ST. PATRICK
PARTNERSHIP CENTER

5

1
HONG KONG SCIENCE PARK

2
HESC

3
SOURTERN TIER LIBRARY SYSTEM

4
SHOPA FOUNDATION FOR EDUCAT-
IONAL EXCELLENCE

5
ST PATRICK PARTNERSHIP CENTER

6
SMITHSONIAN STUDY TOURS

7
EDUCATION BROADCASTING SYSTEM

8
CLASS OF 2001

HESC

2

SMITHSONIAN
STUDY TOURS

6

CareGiver

3

EBS

7

SHOPA™
Foundation for Educational Excellence

4

CLASS OF
2001

8

1
THE LINUS PAULING INSTITUTE

2
TODDLER LEARNING CENTER

3
THE FAMILY ARENA

4
FAST FORWORD

5
GUIDANCE

6
BREAK POINT BOOKS & MORE

7
SUCCESS SYSTEMS

The Linus Pauling Institute

1

guidance

5

fast forword™

4

TLC

Toddler Learning Center

2

break point Books & More

6

THE FAMILY ARENA™

3

SUCCESS SYSTEMS

7

new!

Hopscotch Hill School™

1

MONTEVALLO · FALCONS ·

2

COLLEGE OF AERONAUTICS

3

temple

4

KEYS SCHOOL

5

6

1
HOPSCOTCH HILL SCHOOL

2
UNIVERSITY OF MONTEVALLO F-ALCONS

3
COLLEGE OF AERONAUTICS

4
TEMPLE

5
KEYS SCHOOL

6
NEW YORK UNIVERSITY SCHOOL O-F CONTINUING AND PROFESSIONAL STUDIES

7
SETON HALL UNIVERSITY 1856

SETON HALL UNIVERSITY™

1 8 5 6

7

1
SUMMIT VIEW SCHOOL

2
UNIVERSITAT KAISERSLAUTERN

3
DEPAUL UNIVERSITY

4
ROCKY MOUNTAIN COLLEGE OF ART & DESIGN

5
JOHNSON & WALES UNIVERSITY

6
CALIFORNIA SCHOOL LEADERSHIP ACADEMY

7
THE UNIVERSITY OF TOLEDO

SUMMIT VIEW SCHOOL

1

4

5

2

6

3

THE UNIVERSITY OF
TOLEDO

7

1

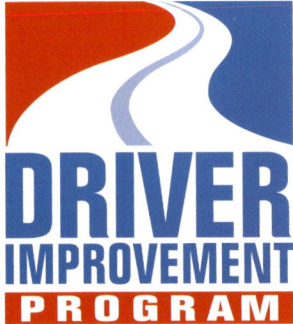

2

DRIVER IMPROVEMENT PROGRAM

3

Concordia
UNIVERSITY·SAINT PAUL

4

GEORGIA SOUTHERN
UNIVERSITY

5

6

BULABAY™

7

1
GRACE ACADEMY

2
BELLA CORIUM

3
DRIVER IMPROVEMENT PROGRAM

4
CONCORDIA UNIVERSITY SAINT PAUL

5
GEORGIA SOUTHERN UNIVERSITY

6
TCU

7
BULABAY

1
STATEN ISLAND JUDO.JUJITSU.D-
OJO

2
EDINBORO UNIVERSITY OF PA

3
HARWOOD CHILDREN'S DAY NURSE-
RY

4
CITY UNIVERSITY OF HONG KONG

5
FEAA

6
NEWBERRY CHILD CARE

7
CENTRAL CITY ACADEMY

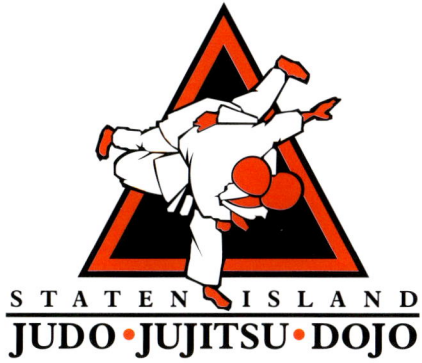

1

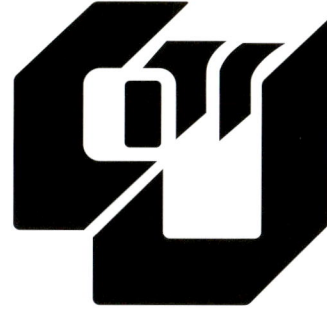

4

FEAA
FACULTATEADE ECONOMIE
SIADMINISTRAREAAFACERILOR

5

2

NEWBERRY
C H I L D C A R E

6

Harwood Children's
Day Nursery

3

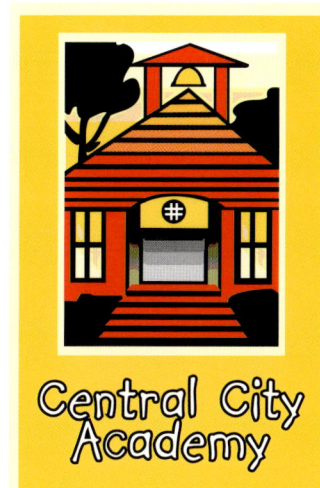

Central City
Academy

7

197

LAVERDONK

1
LAVERDONK DRESSAGE

2
TEMPLE UNIVERSITY

3
MONASH

4
UCL ARTS

5
CALIFORNIA SCHOOL LEADERSHIP ACADEMY

6
NORTHERN ILLINOIS UNIVERSITY FOUNDATION

7
UNIVERSITY OF CALIFORNIA.BERKELEY

1

ELC
Executive
Leadership
Center

5

T

2

3

6

4

BUILD your
FUTURE

7

1
CALIFORNIA COLLEGE OF AYUR-
VEDA

2
KANSAS STATE UNIVERSITY

3
TUMBLEDRUM

4
AMSTERDAM INSTITUTE OF FIN-
ANCE

5
INSTITUTO DE EMPRESA BUSIN-
ESS SCHOOL

6
ACADEMY OF ART COLLEGE

7
UNIVERSITY OF NORTH CAROL-
INA AT CHARLOTTE

4

1

2

3

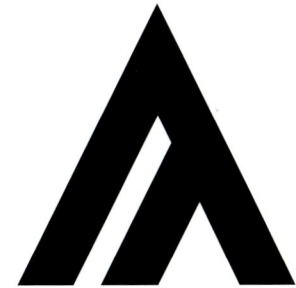

5

Academy of Art College
6

7

199

1

LAMER UNIVERSITY

2

YONEX

3

HUMBER COLLEGE

4

THE DATA WAREHOUSING INSTIT-
UTE

5

DALLAS INDEPENDENT SCHOOL
DISTRICT

6

ESC ROUEN-GRADUATE MANAGEME-
NT SCHOOL

7

WINSOR PILATES

YONEX ®

2

ESC ROUEN

6

WINSOR PILATES ™

7

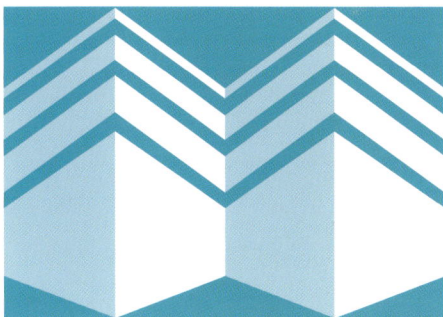

1
WESTERN CULINARY INSTITUTE

2
APPLIED GLOBAL UNIVERSITY

3
JIM MCLEAN GOLF SCHOOLS

4
THE COLLEGE OF NEW ROCHELLE

5
CCI PARIS

6
LIVINGSTON COLLEGE

7
BMW PERFORMANCE CENTER DELI-
VERY

WESTERN CULINARY INSTITUTE

1

CNR Wisdom for life.
The College of New Rochelle

4

C C I PARIS

5

APPLIED GLOBAL UNIVERSITY

2

LIVINGSTON COLLEGE
Shaping Our Community

6

JIM McLEAN GOLF SCHOOLS

3

BMW
Performance Center Delivery

7

SOPEA

1

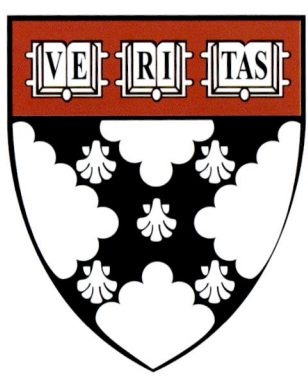

2

VE RI TAS

3

El Paso
Independent
School District

4

5

™

1
SOPEA

2
SAFE PASSAGE

3
HARVARD UNIVERSITY

4
EL PASO INDEPENDENT SCHOOL
DISTRICT

5
SIX SIGMA ACADEMY

6
CENTRAL PARK DANCE

7
TRINITY SCHOOL

Central Park dance

6

Trinity School

7

1
BOLD LIONS CREATIVE ARTS
EDUCATION

2
HANSUNG UNIVERSITY

3
SWINGLAB

4
CONTINUING EDUCATION

5
GIBBS

6
ACHIEVE GLOBAL

7
POLNDEXTER MINISTRIES.INC

BOLD LIONS
Creative Arts Education

1

4

gibbs

5

2

achieveglobal

6

SWINGLAB™

3

Polndexter Ministries. Inc.

7

203

ATTENTION
ALL ANIMALS!

1

2

PACE
UNIVERSITY

3

CARE & TIME
PET SITTING PROFESSIONALS, INC.

4

WISCONSIN REAL
ESTATE ACADEMY

5

West Virginia University

Department of
CHEMISTRY

6

The Learning Practice

7

Kadet
Kindergarden

8

1
ATTENTION ALL ANIMALS!

2
FIRST CLASS CHILD CARE INC

3
PACE UNIVERSITY

4
CARE & TIME PET SITTING
PROFESSIONALS.INC

5
WISCONSIN REAL ESTATE ACADEMY

6
DEPARTMENT OF CHEMISTRY. WEST
VIRGINIA UNIVERSITY

7
THE LEARNING PRACTICE

8
KADET KINDERGARDEN

1
FUTURE KIDS

2
LEARNING TREE INTERNATIONAL

3
AXIOM TRAINING INC

4
MINDSTEP

5
NETG

6
BOWES LEADERSHIP GROUP

7
SPOKANE SKILLS CENTER

8
TOTAL TRAINING

SwitchedOn
Language Arts™

1

NETg ®

Anytime, Anywhere Learning ®

5

Learning Tree ®
International

2

6

3

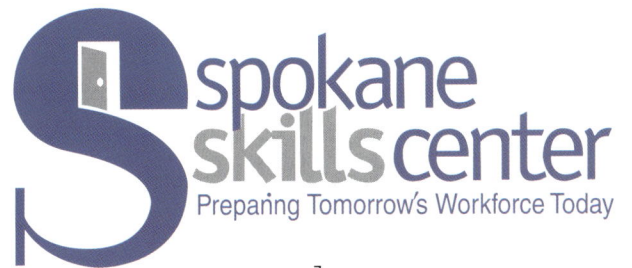
spokane
skills center
Preparing Tomorrow's Workforce Today

7

mindstep

4

TOTAL TRAINING

8

Leadership Lancaster
Developing Leaders for the Future

1

NLP
Seminars Nederland

5

SCT®

2

Root_Learning_® _Inc._

6

TOTAL TRAINING

3

7

WILSON LEARNING

4

THE
LEARNING
ACADEMY
Knowledge to Succeed

8

1
LEADERSHIP LANCASTER

2
SCT

3
TOTAL TRAINING

4
WILSON LEARNING

5
NLP SEMINARS NEDERLAND

6
ROOT LEARNING INC

7
TOUCH VICTORIA

8
THE LEARNING ACADEMY

1
PEER 3

2
CWNP

3
FELDENKRAIS PROFESSIONAL

4
ASTD

5
ITS

6
WORLDWIDE JAVA TRAINING & M—
ENTORING

7
DALE CARNEGIE TRAINING

8
OVERLAND

1

5

6

2

3

7

4

8

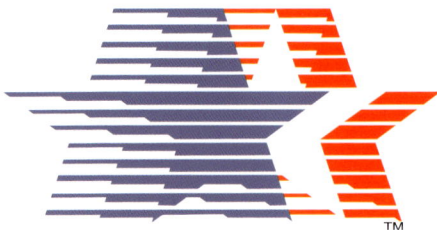

1

2

NAGANO
1 9 9 8

3

Sydney 2000 ™©

4

LA2012

5

SALT LAKE 2002 ™

6

torino 2006 ™

7

1
2002 WINTER OLYMPICS

2
LOS ANGELES 1984

3
NAGANO 1998

4
SYDNEY 2000

5
LOS ANGELES 2012 OLYMPIC BID

6
SALT LAKE 2002

7
TORINO 2006

1
NEW YORK'98 GOODWILL
GAMES

2
AMATEAR ATHLETICS

3
CENTRAL PARK CHALLENGE

4
X GAMES,LOS ANGELES

5
OLYMPIC WORLD

6
1999 SPECIAL OLYMPICS WORLD G-
AMES NORTH CAROLINA

1

4

2

5

3

6

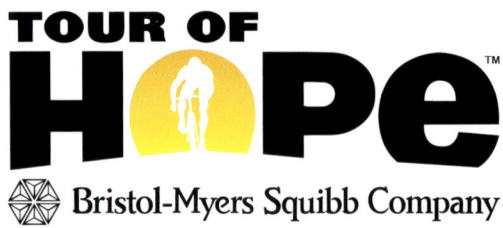

CYCLE OF HOPE™

1

TOUR OF HOPE™
Bristol-Myers Squibb Company

2

3

4

America's
Walk for Diabetes℠
presented by
EQUAL
SWEETENER

5

AVON
RUNNING
Global Women's Circuit

AVON the company for women

6

Boston New York
AIDS Ride 4

7

1
CYCLE OF HOPE

2
TOUR OF HOPE

3
UPTOWN RUN

4
RUN FOR CHRIST

5
AMERICA'S WALK FOR DIABETES

6
AVON RUNNING

7
BOSTON NEW YORK AIDS RIDE

1
FIS ALPINE WORLD SKI CHAMPI-
ONSHIPS BORMIO 2005 LOMBARDIA

2
US OPEN TENNIS CHAMPIONSHIP

3
BRESNAN

4
LUTHERAN CHARITY 5km

5
DEEP ELLUM DASH

6
IKON CLASSIC

7
STEEPLE CHASE

1

4

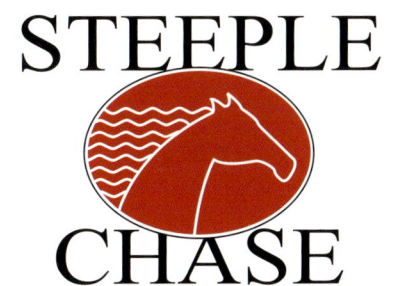

5

2

6

3

7

DONG-A INTERNATIONAL MARATHON RACE

1

PCT

2

SUNSET TENNIS CLASSIC

3

NAPUS UT '01 WENDOVER

4

ALL AMERICAN HIGH SCHOOL BASKETBALL GAME
25th Anniversary Boys Game & Inaugural Girls Game
McDONALD'S

5

AMERICA'S CUP
2003 NEW ZEALAND

6

US OPEN OF SURFING
HUNTINGTON BEACH

7

Vision 2003

8

1
DONG-A INTERNATIONAL MARATH-
ON RACE

2
PRO CYCLING TOUR

3
SUNSET TENNIS CLASSIC

4
NAPUS

5
ALL AMERICAN HIGH SCHOOL BA-
SKETBALL GAME

6
AMERICA'S CUP 2003 NEW ZEAL-
AND

7
US OPEN OF SURFING

8
VISION 2003

1
NATIONAL COMPETITIVE GOLF T-
OUR

2
JAMAICA ONE LIVE CLASSIC

3
JAMAICA ONE LIVE CLASSIC

4
FIELD'S CLASSIC

5
85TH PGA CHAMPIONSHIP OAK H-
ILL

6
BENTON SHIPP GOLF TOURNAMENT

7
AT&T STEVEN A.COX CHARITY C-
LASSIC

4

1

5

2

6

3

7

213

JUNIOR
LEAGUE
OF JACKSON

1

St. Louis
BLUES

25
YEARS

5

1
JUNIOR LEAGUE OF JACKSON

2
AMERICAN YOUTH SOCCER ORGAN-
IZATION FOUNDED 1964

3
WCBF-WORLD CHILDREN'S BASEB-
ALL

4
MINOR LEAGUE BASEBALL

5
ST.LOUIS BLUES.NHL

6
DALLAS MAVERICKS

7
ATLANTA HAWKS

AMERICAN YOUTH SOCCER ORGANIZATION

AY
SO

FOUNDED 1964

2

WCBF

3

6

4

ATLANTA HAWKS

7

1
PITTSBURGH PENGUINS

2
ALEXANDER DAWSON SCHOOL MAS-
COT LAS VEGAS Alexander

3
NEW YORK LIBERTY

4
MILWAUKEE RACQUETEERS

5
ST.JOHN'S UNIVERSITY

6
PACIFIC TIGERS

7
NEW YORK KNICKS

1

2

3

4

5

6

7

215

US SKI TEAM

1

helena pentathlon

4

US SKI TEAM ®

2

5

ELITE HOOPS

6

3

7

1
US SKITEAM

2
US SKITEAM

3
US SNOWBOARDTEAM

4
HELENA PENTATHLON LIONS SWI-
M TEAM

5
BLACK LABEL

6
ELITE HOOPS

7
WICHITA STATE UNIERSITY ME-
N'S CREW TEAM

1
METO

2
MLSPA

3
COBRAS SOCCER

4
WOMEN'S UNITED SOCCER ASSOC-
IATION

5

6
ATLANTA FLAMES HOCKEY

7
CHARLOTTE HEAT

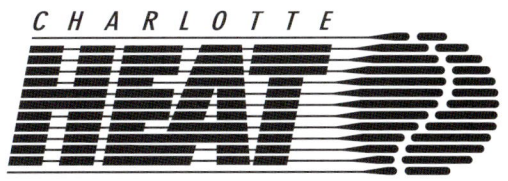

8
BOWLING TEAM

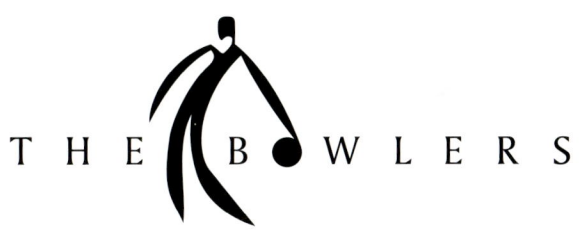

1

5

2

6

3

7

4

8

ST. LOUIS
Rams

1

Steelers

2

SUPER BOWL XXXVI
E✳TRADE
FINANCIAL
HALFTIME SHOW

3

ATLANTA
FALCONS

4

ny

GIANTS.COM

5

6

LIONS

7

1
ST. LOUIS RAMS

2
STEELERS

3
E TRADE

4
ATLANTA FALCONS

5
GIANTS

6
MOORE & ASSOCIATES

7
LIONS

1
DALLAS COWBOYS FOOTBALL

2
CAROLINA PANTHERS

3
SEAHAWKS

4
NEW ENGLAND PATRIOTS

5
TENNESSEE TITANS

6
2001 SEATTLE BOWL

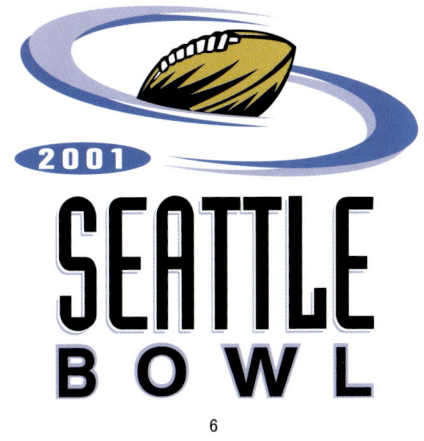

7
BILLS

1

2

3

4

5

6

7

1
KENTUCKY HORSE PARK

2
CEDAR GREEK PLANTATION

3
MOUNTAINEER RACE TRACK

4
RICHMOND RACEWAY

5
GUARANSKI SNOW SUMMIT

6
WINTER NET

7
BIG SKY MONTANA

8
TIGER SCHULMANN'S KARATE

1

WiNTERNET
6

Huffman Arabians

Cedar Creek Plantation
2

3

4

BIG SKY
MONTANA
7

Guaranski
S N O W   S U M M I T
5

TIGER
SCHULMANN'S
KARATE
8

1
VICTORIAN INSTITUTE OF SPORT

2
THE ZONE SPORT SPLEX

3
HIGH DIVE

4
BUCK NAKED BILLIARDS

5
FINS PHILADELPHIA

6
PITTSBURGH SPORTS FESTIVAL

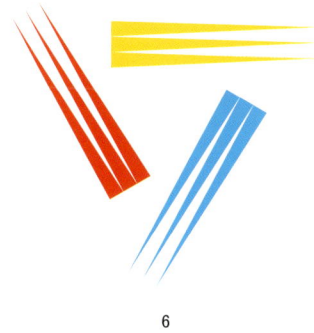

7
PIVOTAL

8
THREE RIVERS STADIUM

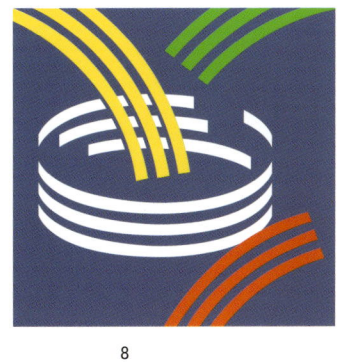

1

5

2

6

3

7

4

8

221

LANCE ARMSTRONG
F O U N D A T I O N

1

4

1
LANCE ARMSTRONG FOUNDATION

2
SAN ANTONIO SPORTS FOUNDAT-
ION

3
SPORTS LAB

4
LA SPORTS COUNCIL

5
RAND MCNALLY

6
IRSA—INTERNATIONAL RAQUET
SPORTS ASSOCIATION

7
MERIDIAN PARTNERS

SAN ANTONIO

SPORTS

FOUNDATION

2

5

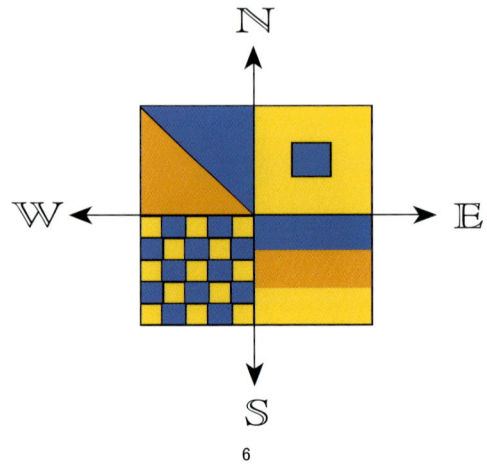

N

W ← → E

S

6

3

M E R I D I A N   P A R T N E R S

7

1
CROSS CREEK GOLF CLUB

2
MOTHER HEN SOFTWARE

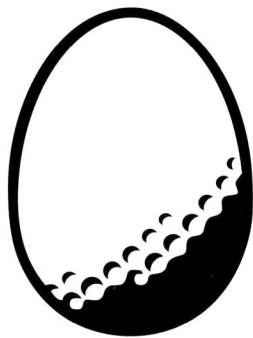

3
KO'OLAU GOLF CLUB

4
GARRISON SPORTS CENTER

5
ST JAMES BAY

6
LEWIS & CLARK GOLF TRAIL

7
J-GOLF FOR NEXTAGE

1

2

3

4

5

6

7

223

1

SPINEZI™

5

1
K2 SKIS

2
K2 SNOWBOARDS

3
ATOMIC SPORT EQUIPMENT

4
SPEED

5
SPINEZI

6
K2 SNOWBOARDS

7
PLAYERS INC

8
CHALLENGE INTERNATIONAL

SNOWBOARDS

2

K2
Snowboards

6

Atomic
Sport Equipment

3

PLAYERS INC

7

S P E E D

4

CHALLENGE
INTERNATIONAL™

8

1
CONVERSE BASKETBALL

2
CHEETAH RECREATIONAL EQUIPM—
ENT

3
LA GEAR

4
ROBINSON RACING PRODUCTS

5
MARKET SKATEBOARDS

6
EKTEION

7
GTRO

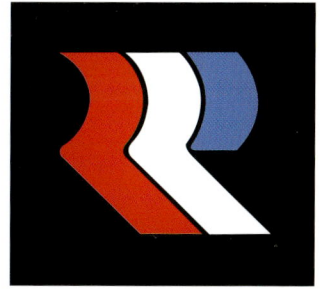

4

1

5

2

6

light GEAR

3

GIRO

7

1
CITY OF SAN ANTONIO OFFICE O-
F CULTURAL AFFAIRS

2
ACN 10th ANNIVERSARY

3
WEST VIRGINIA DIVISION OF CU-
LTURE AND HISTORY

4
CHUNHYANG FESTIVAL

5
CESSNA

6
OFFICIAL SYMBOL FOR THE U.S
BICENTENNIAL

7
2003 CULTUREFEST

CITY OF SAN ANTONIO
OFFICE OF CULTURAL AFFAIRS

1

2

3

CHUNHYANG
FESTIVAL

4

75 · YEARS ·
Cessna
ONE SURE THING

5

Official symbol
for the U.S.
Bicentennial:

6

SMITHSONIAN MAGAZINE'S
2003
CultureFest

7

227

doug baldwin · writer ·

JEWISH CENTER
for Arts and Culture

2

1776

3

U.S. AIR FORCE

5
0

1947-1997

4

honoris causa

6

WOMEN S
HISTORY MONTH

7

1
DOUG BALDWIN WRITER

2
JEWISH CENTER FOR ARTS AND
CULTURE

3
1776

4
U.S.AIR FORCE

5
ARTISTREE

6
HONORIS CAUSA

7
WOMEN'S HISTORY MONTH

1
SUMMER FEST

2
PRAIRIE FEST

3
HARRISON SMITH CYBERSTYLIST

4
DIGITAL ART DIRECTORY

5
SKIRBALL CULTUERAL CENTER

6
KY GUILD OF ARTISTS & CRAFT-SMEN

7
THE SAUSALITO ART FESTIVAL

summer*fest*

1

4

SKIRBALL CULTURAL CENTER

5

2

6

cyberstylist*

3

7

1

1
JAZZ'S ALIVE

2
LIVE BROADWAY

3
RAINBOW BABIES & CHILDRENS'H–
OSPITAL

4
MUSIC IN WOODS

5
MUSIC FESTIVAL

6
WICHITA RIVER FESTIVAL

7
JAZURA ENTERTAINMENT

ACURA MUSIC FESTIVAL DESTINATION NEW ORLEANS

5

LIVE BROADWAY

2

Rainbow Cottages for Kids

3

WICHITA RIVER FESTIVAL

6

4

JAZURA ENTERTAINMENT

7

1
MUNICIPAL FLOW PROMOTIONS

2
RUBIN POSTAER DIRECT/ACURA

3

4
MONTEREY COWBOY POERRY

5
NOKIA5100 CORETOUR SPORTS &
MUSIC FESTIVAL

6
RIVERFRONT CONCERTS

7
ONE WORLD MUSIC

1

4

2

5

6

3

7

Continental Harmony
NEW MUSIC FOR THE MILLENNIUM
1

2

dj *Spiller*
groovejet
3

4

MICHELLE SHOCKED
5

ACE
OF JACKS
6

KENNY
7

8

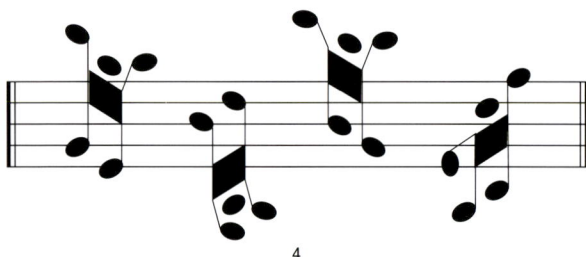

1
CONTINENTAL HARMONY

2
RUSSIAN–AMERICAN MUSIC ASS-
OCIATION

3
DJ SPILLER

4
INTERNATIONAL MUSIC NETWORK

5
SINGER.SONGWRITER MICHELLE
SHOCKED

6
ACE OF JACKS

7
KENNY G/ARTISTA RECORDS

8
TARGET MUSIC RESEARCH

1
RICHMOND BALLET

2
PASADENA CIVIC BALLET

3
BOSTON BALLET

4
JENNY WOODS DANCE

5
CILY BADET OF HOUSTON

6
PITTBURGH DANCE COUNCIL

7
FORT WAYNE BALLET

RICHMOND BALLET

1

JENNY WOODS DANCE

4

OF HOUSTON

5

Pasadena Civic Ballet

2

6

3

Fort Wayne Ballet

7

1

5

1
DALLAS SYMPHONY ORCHESTRA

2
ST. PETER'S COMMUNITY CHOIR

3
SAN FRANCISCO SYMPHONY

4
GREATER DALLAS CHILDREN'S CHORUS

5
ROCK AND ROLL HALL OF FAME & MUSEUM

6
PITTSBURG SYMPHON

7
SEATTLE SYMPHONY

ST. PETER'S COMMUNITY CHOIR

2

PITTSBURG SYMPHON

6

SAN FRANCISCO SYMPHONY

3

4

Seattle Symphony

7

1
BONE DADDY & THE BLUES SHAK-
ERS

2
THE SAMBISTAS

3
SESAME PLACE

4
ESTONIA CHOIR

5
AUSTRALIAN SYMPHONY ORCHEST-
RA

6
CIRCUS BOYS

7
STREET CORNER

1

2

3

4

5

6

7

3RD SMASH YEAR
New York

1

EXODUS

5

1
THE BEAUTY AND BEAST

2
CHICAGO

3
FAME ON 42 ND STREET

4
THE LION KING

5
EXODUS

6
THE SCARLET PIMPERNEL

7
MAN OF LA MANCHAL

CHICAGO

THE MUSICAL

2

FAME
ON 42ND STREET

3

The Scarlet Pimpernel

6

THE LION KING

4

Man of La Mancha

7

1

2
THE BENEDUM CENTER FOR THE
PERFORMING ARTS

3
JAMES HYMAN FINE ART

4
VITAL FORMS "1940–1960"

5
POST PICASSO

6
ACTIVE ARTS

7
M & A COLLECTIONS

1

4

POST **PICASSO** ™

5

2

6

M&A COLLECTIONS

7

3

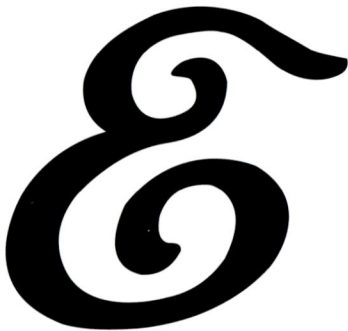

1

2

3

Avante

4

5

BACK STAGE THEATER

6

7

1
PARAMOUNT THEATER

2
EUROARTE

3
KRASTIU SARAFOFF-CHILDRENS T-
HEATRE

4
AVANTE

5
PEACOCK MUSIC STUDIO

6
BACK STAGE THEATER

7
THE SAN DAMIANO PLAYERS

1
SKUP/GLEDALISCE

2
THE OLD GLOBE THEATER

3
PLAYERS THEATRE

4
GEORGIA O'KEEFFE MUSEUM

5
MARK BERGSMA GALLERY

6
ACT THEATRE

7
RADIO CITY

1

O'K

4

mark
bergsma
G A L L E R Y

5

2

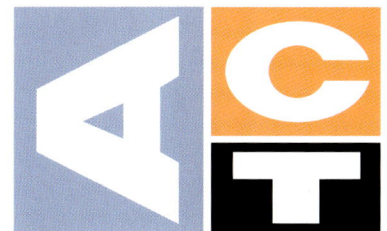

6

ACT
THEATRE

ASSASSINS

3

RADIO CITY
ENTERTAINMENT™

7

Clever Content™

1

eLustro
Agendas

2

winstarinteractive
M E D I A
THE PLACE FOR INTERNET MEDIA BRANDS

3

Carat Interactive

4

CARTA
INTERACTIVE

5

6

Herald Media Inc

7

1
CLEVER CONTENT FROM ALCHEME-DIA

2
MEDIA ENGINE

3
WINSTAR INTERACTIVE MEDIA

4
CARAT INTTERACTIVE

5
CARTA INTERACTIVE

6
INSTITUTE FOR MEDIA ARTS

7
HERALD MEDIA INC

1
EMBASSY COMMUNICATIONS

2
NEW CHANNEL INC.

3
AO ATLANTIC

4
TURNER

5
TELDEC

6
JUXTA MEDIA

7
REUTERS

1

4

NewChannel™ Inc.

2

T E L D E C

5

JUXTA
M E D I A

6

ATLANTIC

3

REUTERS

7

241

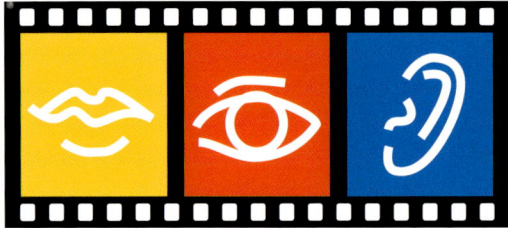

1

2

3

4

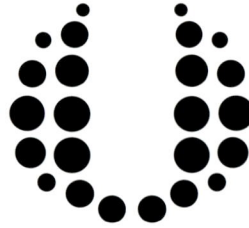

5

6

7

1
DUBAI MEDIA CITY

2
ACTERNA

3
WWW.ZDNET.COM

4
HOOK MEDIA

5
CMP UNITED BUSINESS MEDIA

6
V LAB

7
MACRO MEDIA

1
ONE MEDIA PLACE

2
FREEDOM TECHNOLOGY MEDIA GR-
OUP

3
WWW.USA NETWORK.COM

4
E-MEDIA

5
BOSTON MEDIA CORPORATION

6
PENTON TECHNOLOGY MEDIA

7
DAVIS MEDIA AND PROMOTIONS

8
CHARTER MEDIA

ONE
MEDIA
PLACE

1

E-MEDIA

4

BOSTON MEDIA
CORPORATION

5

Penton

6

Freedom
Technology
Media Group

2

DAVIS MEDIA & PROMOTIONS

7

USA

3

Charter
Media

8

243

V I R T U A L I S

1

2

C X O   M E D I A   I N C.

3

RHIZOME.ORG

4

5

1
VIRTUALIS

2
KINETIKS MEDIA

3
CXO MEDIA INC.

4
RHIZOME ORG

5
FUSION MEDIA

6
DIGITAL MEDIA

7
SIMON LIVE MEDIA NETWORK

Digital_Media_ L.L.P.

6

SIMON **LIVE MEDIA**
N E T W O R K ™

7

1
INNOVATIVE RESEARCH

2
YOUTH STREAM

3
REALTIME MEDIA

4
DIGITAL MEDIA

5
VECTOR MEDIA

6
THE PPI GROUP

7
TICKETS NOW.INC

8
HYDROGEN MEDIA

1

DIGITAL
media

4

5

YOUTHSTREAM

2

THE PPI GROUP

6

TICKETS
now
MEDIA SERVICES

7

3

HYDROGENMEDIA

8

245

YAK CENTRAL
1

GOLF TV
2

EUREEKA'S CASTLE
3

DORA the EXPLORER
4

Blue's Clues ™
5

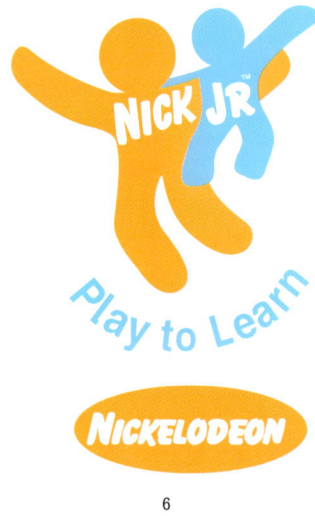
NICK JR Play to Learn
NICKELODEON
6

cityview TV
7

ZOOM ZOOM
ITS CHILD'S PLAY!
8

1
YAK CENTRAL

2
BBS/GOLF TV

3
EUREEKA'S CASTLE

4
NICK JR DORA THE EXPLORER

5
NICK JR BLUE'S CLUES

6
NICKELODEON

7
CITYVIEW TV

8
ZOOM ZOOM

1
GREAT INK

2
VH1 MUSIC FIRST

3
BET ON JAZZ

4
SOPRANOS

5
BIFF HENDERSON OF THE LATE
SHOW WITH DAVID LETTERMAN

6
VT ENTERTAINMENT

7
«BUSINESS 2.0» ECONOMICS

8
ABC SPORTS

1

5

2

6

3

7

4

8

1

CNBC

5

2

Turner Sports

6

3

4

7

1
TNT

2
TLC

3
BET

4
BRAVO

5
CNBC

6
TURNER SPORTS

7
COMEDY CENTRAL

1
PBS THE BUSINESS CHANNEL

2
RCN

3
FX

4
TCM

5
TBS

6
CBS

7
GROOVE TELEVISION

8
MUCHMUSIC USA

PBS
THE BUSINESS CHANNEL SM

1

TBS
SUPERSTATION

5

RCN SM

2

6

FX
please watch responsibly

3

groovetelevision

7

TCM

4

muchmusic usa

8

1

5

2

6

NICKELODEON

3

MR SHOWBIZ

7

4

8

1
FOX NEWS CHANNEL

2
CBS SPORTS LINE

3
NICKELODEON

4
COURT TV

5
HOOPS TV.COM

6
PLAYBOY TV

7
MR SHOWBIZ

8
NICKELODEON

1
NFL

2
VH1 SATELLITE RADIO

3
NFL

4
LINKS ILLUSTRATED TELEVISION

5
E!

6
HOME & GARDEN TELEVISION

7
ESPN 2

8
ON 24

1

5

2

6

3

7

4

8

1

2

3

4

5

6

7

8

1
NFL

2
TNN

3
LIVE TV

4
STYLE

5
CABLENET

6
SCREEN FOR SUCCESS

7
PARDON THE INTERRUPTION

8
THE NATIONAL NETWORK (TNN)

1
MTM FAMILY NETWORK

2
PBS KIDS

3
FOX BROADCASTING

4
SPACE NEEDLE

5
XM

6
SPARK TELEVISION

7
CNN

1

4

SEE IT ON PBS KIDS™

2

SATELLITE RADIO

5

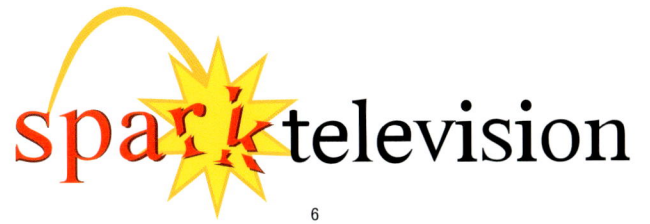

6

3

7

SIRIUS

1

2

3

4

5

6

7

8

1
SIRIUS SATELLITE RADIO

2
HBO

3
SKY TV

4
ESPRI TV

5
Q101 RADIO

6
KHCV TV SEATTLE

7
LOCAL TV

8
WB FAMILY ENTERTAINMENT

1
ASDA

2
LONE STAR RADIO NETWORK

3
TOKYO BROADCASTING SYSTEM

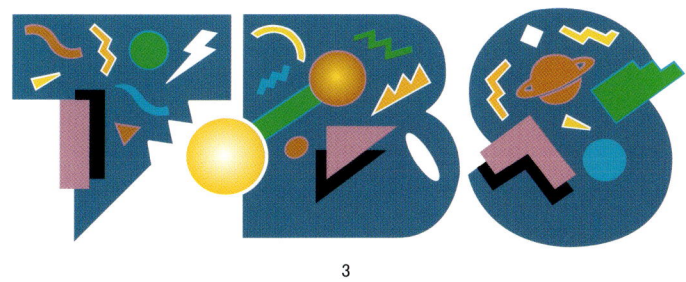

4
INTERNATIONAL BOADCAST SYSTE-
MS.INC

5
SUNNY 101.5FM

6
CHILDREN'S BROADCASTING CORP.

7
CHILDREN'S BROADCASTING CORP.

1

4

5

2

6

3

7

255

BENLTOR
FILMGROUP

1

NILES
moTION
PICTURES

2

3

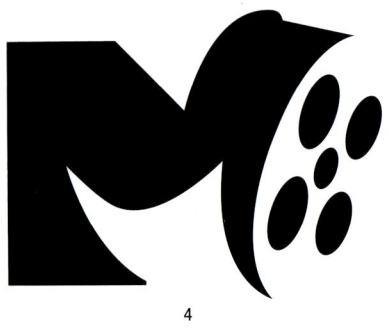

4

5

1
BENLTOR FILM GROUP

2
NILES MOTION PICTURES

3
REGINA PUBLIC LIBRARY FILMM
THEATRE

4
MOBILE VISION

5
WOMEN'S BOOK OF CHANGES

6
MOVING PICTURES EDITIONAL

7
CINEROM

6

CINEROM

7

1
JUNGANG CINEMA

2
MIKE STANLEY FREELANCE VIDEO

3
CINE PLUS

4
GENERAL CINEMA CORPORATION

5
GROTTO FILMS PRODUCTION

6
THE 2002 IFP WEST

7
EVOLUTION FILM & TAPE

1

General
Cinema

4

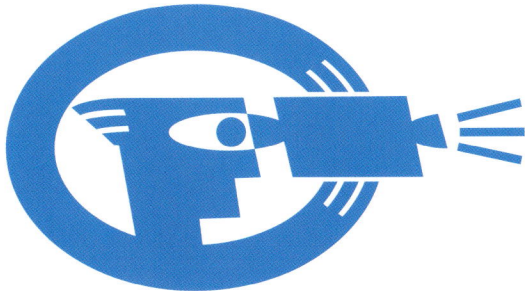

2

5

THE 2002 ifp/west

6

CINE+

3

7

257

PENTAMERICA
PICTURES

1

LADYLIKE
PRODUCTIONS

2

STARZ ENCORE
GROUP

3

Civilian
Pictures, LLC

4

5

6

ci consolidated
film
imaging

7

1
PENTAMERICA PICTURES

2
LADYLIKE PRODUCTIONS

3
STARZ ENCORE GROUP

4
CIVILIAN PICTURES.LLC

5
TULIP FILMS

6
MOTION PROJECTS

7
CONSOLIDATED FILM IMAGING

1
DOLORES PICTURES

2
MONARCH FILMS

3
PLAYER PICTURES LLC

4
MAGIC HOUR PICTURES

5
STORY GARDEN PRODUCTIONS

6
ROADSHOW FILMS

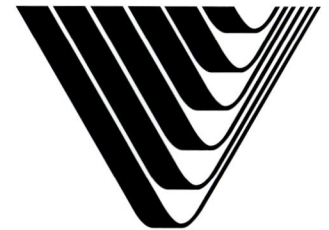

7
K & M PRODUCTIONS

DOLORES
P I C T U R E S

1

MAGIC HOUR
P I C T U R E S

4

2

5

ROADSHOW FILMS

6

Player
PICTURES
LLC

3

KM
PRODUCTIONS

7

259

GRAMERCY
P I C T U R E S

1

TRiBE

[moving]

Pictures

2

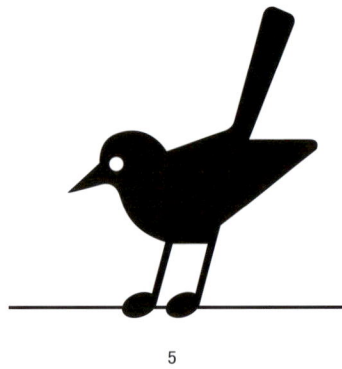

3

4

5

AZALEA FILMS

6

Hindsight Productions, LLC

the future
of the past

7

1
GRAMERCY

2
TRIBE PICTURES

3
SELECT SYNDICATION

4
TONAMT FRANKFURT

5
TEQUILA MOCKINGBIRD

6
AZALEA FILMS

7
HINDSIGHT PRODUCTIONS,LLC

1
ROARING TIGER FILMS

2
HEMISPHERE PRODUCTIONS

3
THE FOOD CHAIN

4
CLINE DAVIS & MANN INC

5
PARAMOUNT

6
SFX ENTERTAINMENT

7
REMBRENT PRODUCTIONS

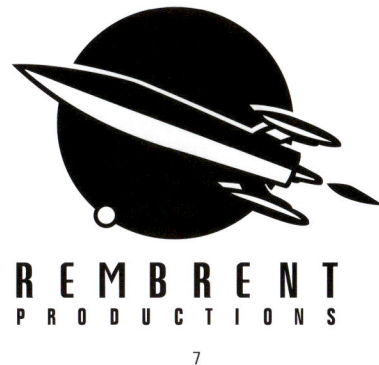

1

4

2

5

6

3

7

1

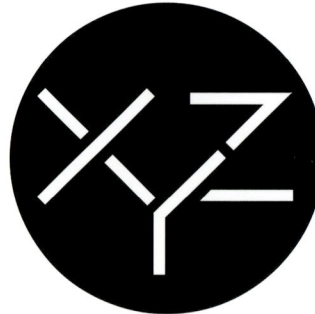

2

3

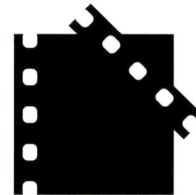

Elaktra Enterlainment

4

XYZ

5

NEW LINE CINEMA

6

.bluehat
M E D I A •••••

7

1
FRENCHBREAD PRODUCTIONS

2
BACK AGAIN PRODUCTIONS

3
CHAPTER ONE PRODUCTIONS

4
ELAKTRA ENTERLAINMENT

5
XYZ PRODUCTIONS

6
NEW LINE CINEMA

7
BLUE HAT MEDIA

1
SHOKT INTERNET PRODUCTIONS

2
ON LIVE!TECHNOLOGIES

3
MACE ENTERTAINMENT

4
CRESCENT MOON ENTERTAINMENT

5
TAKE ONE VIDEO PRODUCTIONS

6
ZENITH

7
PDX ENTERTAINMENT

1

4

5

2

6

3

7

1

2

3

Rocksford
Book Factory

4

Revell

5

6

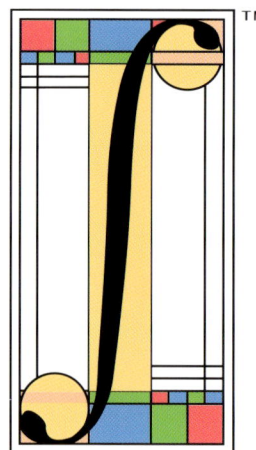

7

1
SLOVENSKA KNJIGA LJUBLJANA

2
BIG PAWS RECORDS

3
QBPL KIDS

4
ROCKSFORD BOOK FACTORY

5
FLEMING H REVELL PUBLISHING

6
SWAN SONGS

7
INTEGRE TECHNICAL PUBLISHING
CO..INC.

1
SEMINARS WITH RACHEL JACOB-
SOHN

2
BROWN DEER PRESS

3
WHAT FUN!

4
SUN LION PRESS

5
WEST GROUP

6
NAC NAC

7
COMMERCIAL PRESS

1

4

WEST GROUP

5

BROWN DEER

PRESS

2

Nac Nac

6

What·Fun!
Fun for your Life!

3

C
COMMERCIAL PRESS

7

265

1

2

funny pages

PRESS

5

LONGDAY BOOKS

3

X

6

INDIE**VIDUAL**

4

MAGIC CARPET

BOOKS

7

1
HAWK'S NEST PUBLISHING

2
SNAKE MUSIC

3
LONGDAY BOOKS

4
INDIE VIDUAL

5
FUNNY PAGE PRESS

6
MUSE X EDITAIONS

7
MAGIC CARPET BOOKS

1
FILE MAKER

2
ECLIPSE INTERACTIVE PUBLISH-
ING.INC

3
NORTH MAIN

4
BALLANTINE BOOK

5
BECKETT HONORS

6
HYPERION

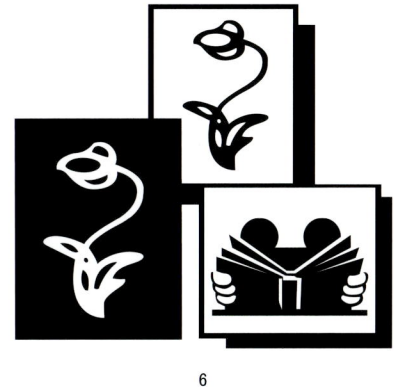

7
DISCIPLE RECORDS

FileMaker®

1

4

Beckett Honors

5

ECLIPSE

INTERACTIVE PUBLISHING, INC.

2

6

21 NORTH MAIN SM

3

DISCIPLE
RECORDS

7

267

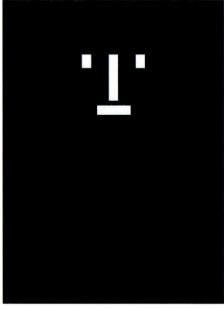

TEXERE

1

EDPRESS

2

GULLIVER
B O O K S

3

M A C M I L L A N
DIGITAL PUBLISHING USA

4

5

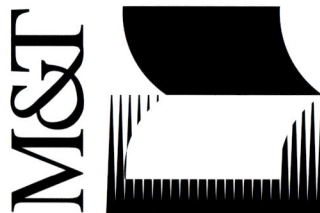

6

M&T BOOKS

7

1
TEXERE

2
EDPRESS

3
GULLIVER BOOKS

4
MACMILLAN DIGITAL PUBLISHI-
NG USA

5
GOLDEN BOOKS FAMILY ENTERTA-
INMENT

6

7
M & T

1
STORY BOX

2
IEEE SPECTRUM

3
IT'S ABOUT TIME

4
CIRCUITS

5
IN 2 BOOKS

6
PEAK EXPERIENCES

7
CTIA WIRELESSI.T.& ENTERTAI-
NMENT 2003

8
FORBES

StoryBox

1

in2books
A Reading Pen Pal Program

5

IEEE
SPECTRUM

2

PEAK
EXPERIENCES
DISCOVER THE GREAT INDOORS.

6

it's about time

3

CTIAWIRELESSI.T. & ENTERTAINMENT 2003

7

4

Forbes
.com

8

1

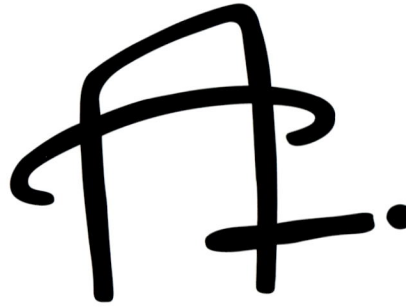

5

2

1
DRAGON TALES

2
COOKING LIGHT ON THE MOVE

3
INFO LINK

4
TIME OPINION LEADERS

5
CIGAR AFCIONADO MAGAZINE

6
TRANSFORM MAGAZINE

7
ATITECH

6

3

4

7

1
CHUCK'S NEWSTAND

2
PC WORLD

3
MEDIA

4
READER'S DIGEST

5
FORBES MAGAZINE

6
OUTSOURCE WORLD

7
THE NEXT FRONTIERS

8 «WIRED»

1

4

5

2000

2

6

7

3

8

songwriter records

1

1
SONGWRITER RECORDS

2
ACOUS TECH

3
NO WAY! RECORDS

4
EAST WEST RECORDS

5
VELLUM POINT

6
BATON RECORDS

7
PURGATONE RECORDS

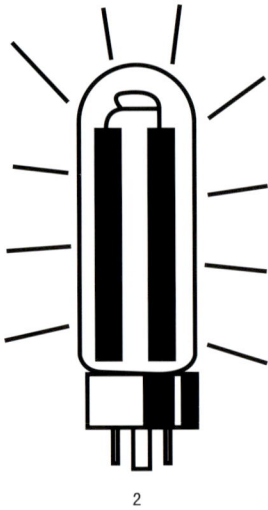

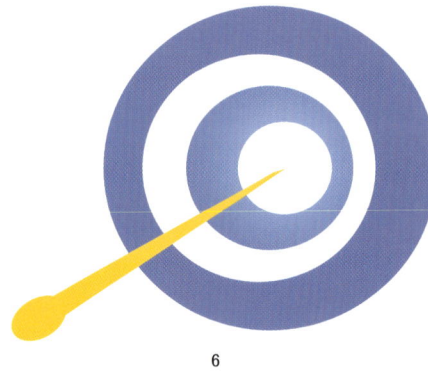

5

2

6

NO WAY! RECORDS
DOT COM

3

ew

eastwest records

4

7

1
MOULIN RECORDINGS

2
SOSODEF RECORDINGS

3
PUMP RECORDS

4
SONGSMITH

5
CD FORCE

6
SAM GOODY

7
VIRGIN RECORDS

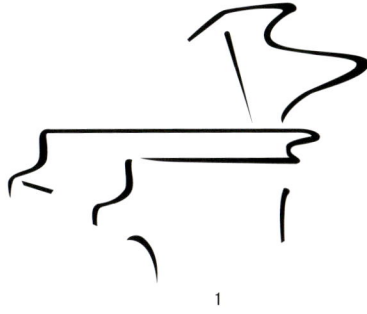

1

S O N G S M I T H

4

2

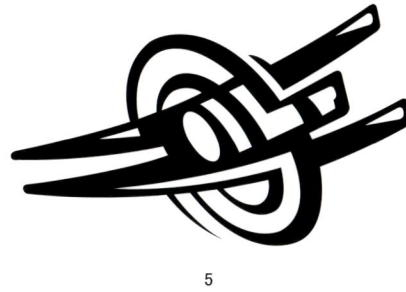

5

6

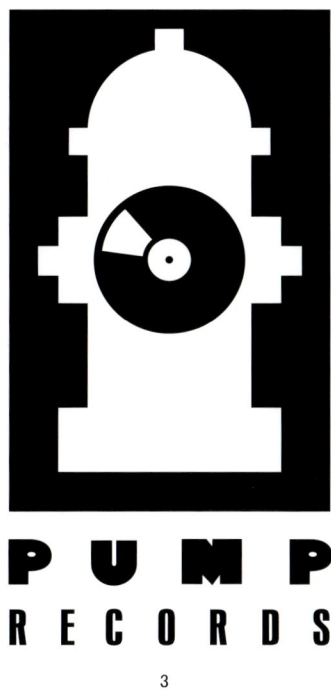

3

7

273

Noir Heaven
Le MovieVille

1

4

1
MOVIEVILLE VIDEO CORPORATION

2
STEREOLAB

3
HOLLYWOOD RECORDS

4
BOCKBUSTER VIDEO

5
BOCKBUSTER VIDEO

6
BOCKBUSTER VIDEO

STEREOLAB

2

SUMMT

5

Hollywood
RECORDS

3

6

DISNEY'S ANIMAL KINGDOM

Disney Online

1

Disney 1.com

2

WALL OF SOUND

3

ESPN.com

4

Disney PRESS

5

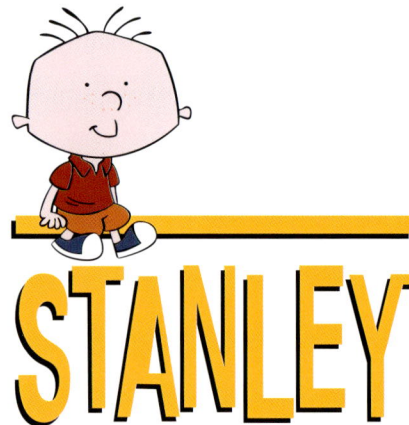

Go.com

6

STANLEY

7

1
DISNEY ONLINE

2
DISNEY 1.COM

3
WALL OF SOUND

4
ESPN.COM

5
DISNEY PRESS

6
GO.COM

7
STANLEY

1
RADIO & DISNEY

2
WALT DISNEY WORLD DOLPHIN

3
VACATION TOGETHER

4
DISNEY PLAY TOY STORY

5
ZAPPING ZONE

6
DISNEY HAND

3

1

4

WALT DISNEY WORLD
DOLPHIN

2

ZAPPING ZONE

5

Disney HAND

6

WALT DISNEY World

1

Disney 75 YEARS

5

1
WALT DISNEY WORLD

2
WALT DISNEY WORLD SWAN

3
DISNEY CRUISE LINE

4
WALT DISNEY FANTASIA 2000

5
DISNEY 75 YEARS

6
DISNEY LAND PARIS-DISNEY

7
MICKEY'S STUFF FOR KIDS

WALT DISNEY WORLD SWAN

2

6

Disney CRUISE LINE

3

FANTASIA 2000

4

MICKEY'S STUFF for kids

7

1
GOVERNORS COMMISSION

2
ACCOUNTING CORNER

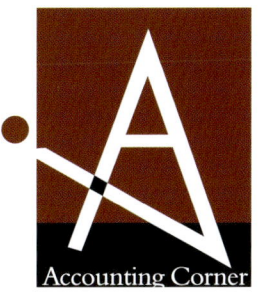

3
ONONDAGA COUNTY REPUBLICAN
PARTY

4
PORT OF MIAMI

5
PUERTO RICO CONVENTION BU-
REAU

6
THE BETTER BUSINESS BUREAU

7
CITY OF CHARLOTTE

8
ATASTE OF ARLINGTON

1

PUERTO RICO
CONVENTION BUREAU

5

Accounting Corner

2

BBB
The Better Business Bureau

6

HALL of FAME
Onondage County Republican Party

3

CHARLOTTE

7

Port of Miami

4

A Taste of Arlington

8

279

THE ROYAL EMBASSY OF SAUDI ARABIA WASHINGTON, D.C.

1

2

3

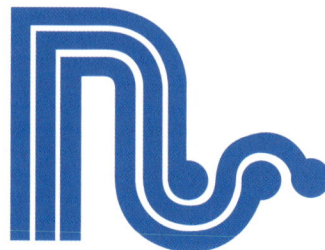

4

Federal Highway Administration
Office of Policy

5

6

7

City of Millville

8

1
THE ROYAL EMBASSY OF SAUDI
ARABIA WASHINGTON.D.C

2
PERSONNEL UNLIMITED

3
MY POOL PAL PLAY TI SAFE

4
US EMPLOYMENT SERVICE DEPT
OF LABOR

5
FEDERAL HIGHWAY ADMINISTR-
ATION

6
CITY OF NIAGARA

7
CITY OF PASADENA

8
CITY OF MILLVILLE

1
BLANK ROME COUNSELORS AT LAW

2
GEMFIRE

3
SUHSB

4
BROBECK

5
MODRALL SPERLING LAWYERS

6
INSTITUTE OF COMPUTER AND
COMMUNICATIONS LAW

7
ACME WILEY.LNC.

8
NIXON PEABODY LLP

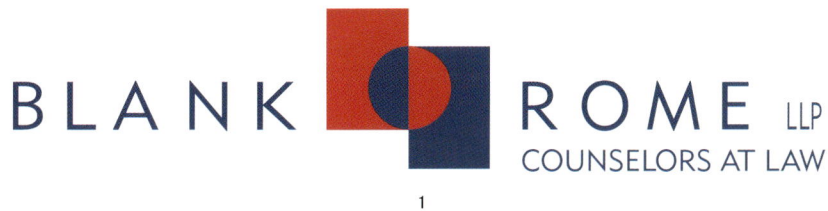

1

2

6

3

7

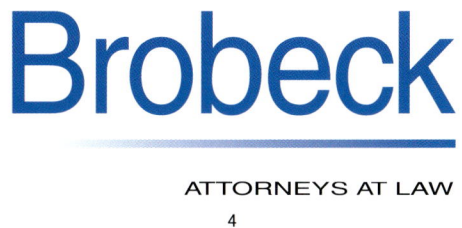

4

5

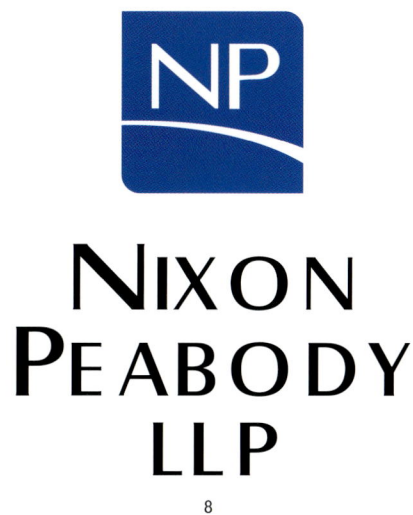

8

SALTWATER CITY

1

2

3

7

4

5

6

OAKVILLE

8

1
SALTWATER CITY

2
DBCC ATTORNEYS AT LAW

3
VICTORY

4
SANTA CLARA VALLEY TRANSPO-
RTATION AUTHORITY

5
MARRIAGE

6
MARRIAGE

7
SALT LAKE CITY-COUNTY HEA-
LTH DEPARTMENT

8
TOWN OF OAKVILLE

1
NARITA CITY

2
CITY OF WICHITA

3
MARTINDALE-HUBBELL

4
PITTSBURGH DEPARTMENT OF CI-
TY PLANNING

5
WINNIPEG LNTERNATIONALCHILD-
REN'S FESTIONAL

6
NY WATERWAY

7
SINGAPORE POLICE FORCE

8
THE SECURITY STORE

1

5

2

6

MARTINDALE-HUBBELL

3

7

4

8

WONJU

1

PorchLight

2

THE CITY OF SPOKANE

3

AIR FORCE RESERVE

4

5

POLETOWN DETROIT

6

WICHITA'S PROMISE SPRING RETREAT

7

1
WONJU CITY

2
SEATTLE HOUSING AUTHORITY

3
THE CITY OF SPOKANE

4
AIR FORCE RESERVE

5
FEMA

6
POLETOWN. DETROIT

7
WICHITA'S PROMISE SPRING RETREAT

MINNESOTA LANDSCAPE ARBORE-
TUM

Minnesota Landscape

ARBORETUM

1

2

3

4

6

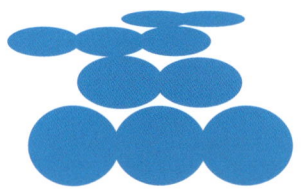

7

4

National Undergroud Railroad
U FREEDOM CENTER

5

8

1
MARKET CENTRAL

2
MT SINAI CHILDREN'S CENTER

3
KANE REGIONAL CENTERKANE

4
MANOMET CENTER FOR CONSERV-
ATION SCIENCES

5
NATIONAL UNDERGROUD RAILRO-
AD FREEDOM CENTER

6
KOREA WATER RESOURCES CORP-
ORATION

7
AMERICAN INDIAN COMMUNITY
CENTER

8
CITY OF HOPE NATIONAL MEDI-
CAL CENTER AND BECKMAN RES-
EARCH INSTITUTE

1
MERCURY CENTER THE CONTER OF
SILLCON VALLEY

2
ALLEN CENTER

3
SAFER

4
KOLL ANAHEIM CENTER

5
AMERICAN EXPRESS

6
ADELAIDE CONVENTION CENTRE
SOUTH AUSTRALIA

7
JPMA

8
NATIONAL SPORTS SCIENCE CE-
NTER

1

Small
Business
Exchange

5

Allen Center

2

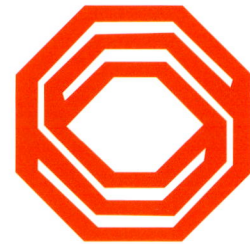

6

3

7

KOLL ANAHEIM CENTER

4

8

1

2

3

5

6

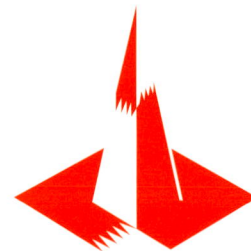

7

8

1
AMERICAN ASSOCIATION OF MU-
SEUMS

2
AMERICAN DIABETES ASSOCIAT-
ION

3
WOMEN FOR WOMEN

4
USA GYMNASTICS

5
DSVC DESIGNER`S CHILI COOK-
OFF

6
COSMETIC ASSOCIATES

7
BAHRAIN PROMOTIONS&MARKETI-
NG BOARD

8
ASP ASSOCIATION OF SURFING-
PROFESSIONALS NORTH AMERICA

1
TODAY'S TRAVELER

2
JEWISH FEDERATION OF ST.LO-
UIS

3
PHILADELPHIA REGISTERED NU-
RSE PRACTITIONER

4
MOTHERS

5
THE CLIMATE INSTITUTE

6
TRUCHAS HYDROLOGIC ASSOC-
IATES

7
YMCK

8
NATIONAL COOPERATIVE EDUCA-
TION PROGRAM

1

5

2

6

3

7

4

8

1

NORTHERN ILLINOIS BOTANICAL SOCIETY

Garden
Glory
Walk & Festival

2

vo1ce

3

MOTHERS'
VOICES
United to end AIDS®

4

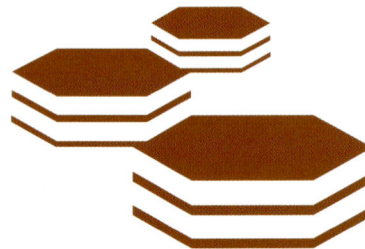

1
STILL
THE
ONE
1

5

6

PARENTS AS TEACHERS

NATIONAL CENTER, INC.

7

1
PACIFICARE MATTERS ON MATE-
RNITY

2
NORTHERN ILLINOIS BOTANICAL
SOCIETY

3
AIGA

4
MOTHERS'VOICES UNITED TO
END AIDS

5
FOOD MARKETING INSTIUTE

6
KOREA VENTURE CAPITAL ASS-
OCIATION

7
PARENTS AS TEACHERS NATIONAL
CENTER INC

1
AVP

2
ROYAL GUIDE DOG ASSOCIATION

3
ADOPT-A-HIGHWAY

4
AMERICA IS ON THE WATER "N-ATIONAL MARINE MANUFACTURERS ASSOCIATION

5
AMERICAN ACADEMY OF COSMETI-C SURCERY

6
SUN SAFETY ALLIANCE BLOCK THE SUN.NOT THE FUN

7
ELECTRIC VEHICLE ASSOCIATION OF THE AMERICAS

avp

1

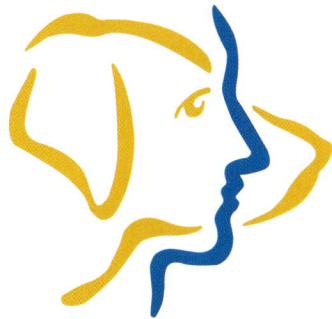

2

ADOPT-A-HIGHWAY

3

America is on the Water

National Marine Manufacturers Association

4

AMERICAN ACADEMY OF COSMETIC SURCERY

5

Sun Safety Alliance℠

Block the Sun, Not the Fun™

6

Electric Vehicle Association of the Americas

7

291

AMERICA'S
C H O I C E

1

CEA

2

Society of
SeniorMarket
Professionals

3

APCOR
Portuguese Cork Association

4

5

The incredible edible egg

American Egg Board
www.aeb.org

6

IDARA

7

1
AMERICA'S CHOICE PROGRAM

2
CONSUMER ELECTRONICS ASSOC-
IATION

3
SOCIETY OF SENIOR MARKET P-
ROFESSIONALS

4
APCOR PORTUGUESE CORK ASS-
OCIATION

5
DISABLEDCHILDREN'S ASSOCIA-
TION OF SAUDI ARABIA

6
AMERICAN EGG BOARD

7
YOUNG PRESIDENTS'ORGANIZA-
TION

1
ASSOCIATION OF GOVERNMENT
ACCOUNTANTS

2
GREENWICH VILLAGE CHAMBER
OF COMMERCE

3
AMERICAN HEART ASSOCIATION

4
YAI NATIONAL INSTITUTE FOR
PEOPLE WITH DISABILITIES N-
ETWORK

5
PETS ARE LOVING SUPPORT

6
CADA

7
BIA BRICK INDUSTRY ASSOCIA-
TION

1

5

2

6

3

7

4

1

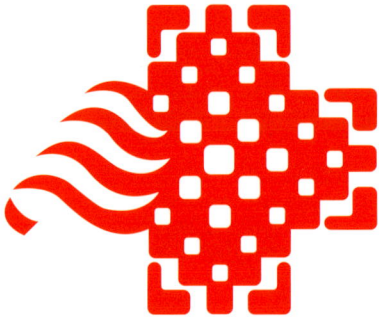

2

3

5

IAAPA

6

4

7

1
ITERNATIONAL ADVERTISING
ASSOCIATION

2
NATIONAL HISPANIC HEALTH C-
OALITION

3
THE ACTORS ENSEMBLE

4
TUCSON ZOOLOGICAL SOCIETY

5
AMERICAN SOCIETY OF PLAST-
IC SURGEONS

6
INTERNATIONAL ASSOCIATION
OF AMUSEMENT PARKS AND AT-
TRACTIONS

7
BCM

1
HAKOSHIKI

2
NCB—NATIONAL CONTRACTORS

3
GOLDEN GLOVES

4
MARTHA MCMILLIAN

5
AWC

6
AMERICAN CANCER SOCIETY

7
AMERICAN ZOO & AQUARIUM AS
SOCIATION

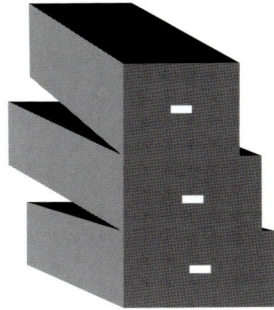

1

2

GOLDEN GLOVES

3

4

5

6

7

1

2

3

5

6

7

4

8

1
TOURETTE SYNDROME ASSOCIAT-
ION.INC

2
HUMANE SOCIETY OF AUSTIN

3
PREPARATORY COMMISSION FOR
THE COMPREHENSIVE NUCLEAR-
TEST-BANTREATY ORGANIZATI-
ON(CTBTO)

4
ASSOCIATION OF INTERNET
PROFESSIONALS

5

6
COALITION FOR MONTANANS
CONCERNED WITH DISABILITIES

7
IGI

8
LITERACY VOLUNTEERS

1
ITCA

2
KANSAS HUMANE SOCIETY

3
HIGH SIERRA PASSPORT TO AD-
VENTURE

4
FRIENDS OF AUBURN /TAHOE
VISTA PLACER COUNTY ANIMAL
SHELTER

5
AIGA

6
HUNTINGTON'S DISEASE SOCIETY
OF AMERICA

7
EUROPEAN BROADCASTING UNION

4

1

5

2

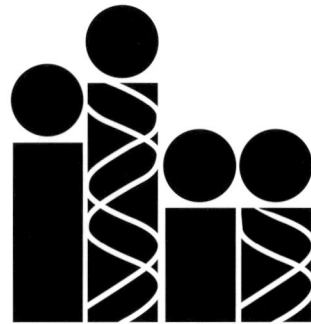

6

3

7

COMPUTERWORLD
IT Executive Summit
series

1

INTERNATIONAL SPACE THEATER CONSORTIUM

2

CANCER*care*®

3

Los Angeles

4

Ifimes

5

6

7

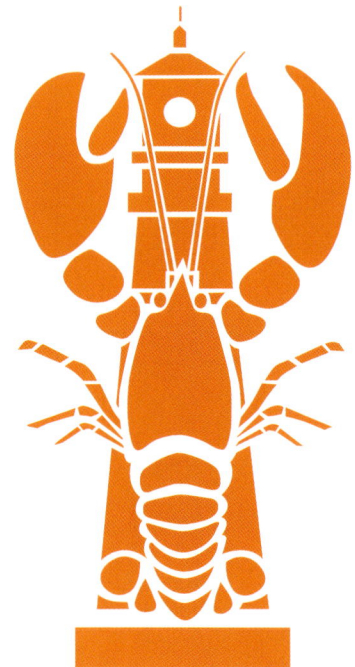

8

1
COMPUTERWORLD IT EXECUTIVE
SUMMIT SERIES

2
INTERNATIONAL SPACE THEATER
CONSORTIUM

3
CANCER CARE

4
LOS ANGELES AREA CHAMBER OF
COMMERCE

5
LFIMES

6
AVON WOMEN OF ENTERPRISE

7
YWCA

8
AIA MAINE-A CHAPTER OF THE
AMERICAN INSTITUTE OF ARC-
HITECTS

1
BUILDERS ALLIANCE

2
GAME DAY

3
PACIFIC EMPLOYERS ORGANIZA-
TION

4
VOLUNT EARS

5
DIGITAL TRAILS

6
AMA

7
WASHINGTON TRAILS ASSOCI-
ATION

1

4

2

5

6

3

7

1

5

1
AMERICAN HUMANE ASSOCIATION

2
PEACE WINDS

3
BICSI

4
BUSINESS COMMITTEE FOR THE ARTS,INC.

5
HEART OF LOS ANGELES YOUTH

6
NEW YORK AMERICAN MARKETING ASSOCIATION

7
WALL ST RISING

2

New York
AMA

6

3

Business Committee for the Arts, Inc.

4

WALL ST

RISING

7

1
WATER KEEPER

2
SHARE OUR VISION

3
OUR EARTH.OUR TOMORROW

4
HEROES FOR THE PLANET

5
EARTH SOURCE

6
THE AMERICAN PAVILION

7
CRISTINA FOUNDATION

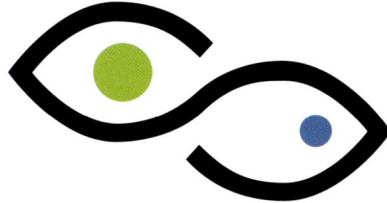

1

Share our Vision

2

**Our earth,
Our tomorrow**

3

HEROES FOR THE PLANET™

4

earthsource℠

POWER FOR A NEW WORLD

5

THE AMERICAN · PAVILION

6

National **Cristina**™
Foundation

7

SAVE AMERICA'S TREASURES
NATIONAL TRUST FOR HISTORIC PRESERVATION

1

2

STAR ALLIANCE

6

3

7

PLAN
INTERNATIONAL

4

KidsPeace ®

8

altrue istic
Easy Website for Non-Profits

5

1
SAVE AMERICA'S TREASURES N-
ATIONAL TRUST FOR HISTORIC
PRESERVATION

2
BIG BROTHER, BIG SISTER IN
NEW YORK CITY

3
INTERNATIONAL STUDIES ASSO-
CIATION

4
PLAN INTERNATIONAL

5
ALTRUE

6
STAR ALLIANCE

7
WORLD TRADE ORGANIZATION

8
KIDS PEACE

1
ALL-AID INTERNATIONAL.INC.

2
WORLD WILDLIFE FUND

3
BOYS & GIRLS CLUBS OF AMER-
ICA

4
THE CROSS-REGIONAL BUSINESS
SCHOOL AEA ALLIANCE

5
IOM INTERNATIONAL ORGANIZA-
TION FOR MIGRATION

6
CLEAN WATER OREGON

7
GIRL SCOUTS

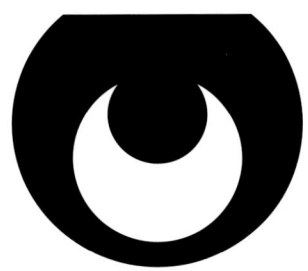

All-Aid
International, Inc.

1

The Cross-Regional Business School
AEA ALLIANCE

4

IOM International Organization for Migration

5

2

6

BOYS & GIRLS CLUBS
OF AMERICA

3

GIRL SCOUTS

7

1

2

3

4

5

6

7

1
ASSE INTERNATIONAL STUDENT
EXCHANGE PROGRAMS

2
FRIENDS OF ANIMALS FRIENDS
FOR LIFE

3
SHOES FOR RUSSIAN SOULS

4
LEARNING LEADERS

5
CANDLES

6
WE WILL NOT FORGET 911

7
COAST RUNNER

1
INTERNATIONAL AMNESTY

2
NOW GLOBAL EMERGENCY.ORG

3
Peace, Love and Harmony

4
RESPECT THE LAND WE LOVE

5
"SAVE"

6
HUMANITY IN ACTION

7
WOMEN'S SPORTS FOUNDATION

1

Students Against Violence Everywhere

SAVE

5

now
Global
emergency.org

2

peace love and HARMONY

3

Humanity In Action
Education, Healthcare, Human Freedom

6

Respect The Land We Love™

4

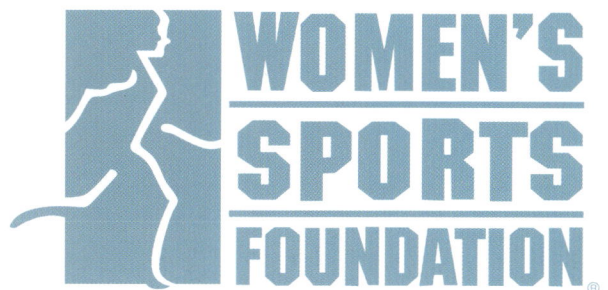

WOMEN'S SPORTS FOUNDATION

7

305

1

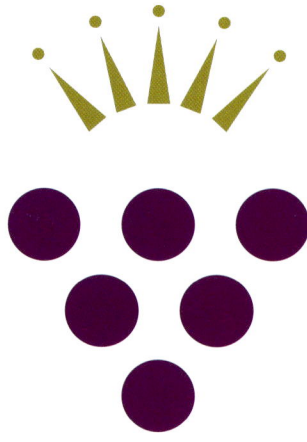

5

1
THE LEARNING ALLIANCE

2
METRO DENVER NETWORK

3
CPRN (CANADIAN POLICY RESE-
ARCH NETWORKS)

4
UDA (UNITED DIGITAL ARTISTS)

5
THE KING RANCH VINEYARD PA-
RTNERSHIP

6
ACCA SOURCE

7
CHICAGO ASSOCIATION OF REA-
LTORS

METRO DENVER NETWORK

2

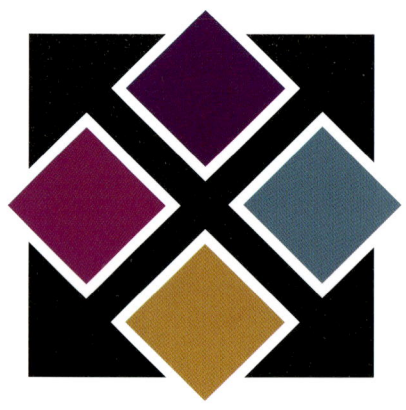

6

3

7

uda **united digital artists**

4

1
THE NATIONAL CONGRESS FOR
NEW POLITICS

2
ICBA—INDEPENDENT COLLEGE
BOOKSTORE ASSOCIATION

3
AUSTRIAN EMBROIDERIES

4
ALLIANCE FOR BETTER CAMPAI-
GNS

5
AMERICAN FEDERATION OF GOV-
ERNMENT EMPLOYEES

6
UJA-FEDERATION OF NEW YORK

7
ASSOCIATION OF MATERNAL &
CHILD HEALTH PROGRAMS

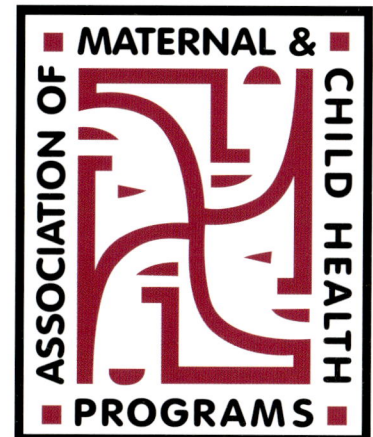

1

4

cba

2

5

UJA-FEDERATION OF NEW YORK

6

AUSTRIAN EMBROIDERIES

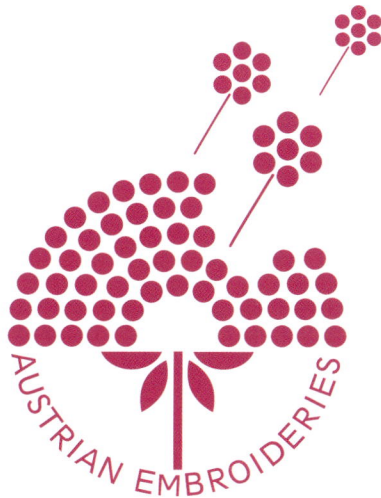

3

ASSOCIATION OF MATERNAL & CHILD HEALTH PROGRAMS

7

1

HeartShare

2

3

Special Singles ONLINE

4

MAKING HEALTH A HUMAN RIGHT

5

mission **POSSIBLE** *music*

6

7

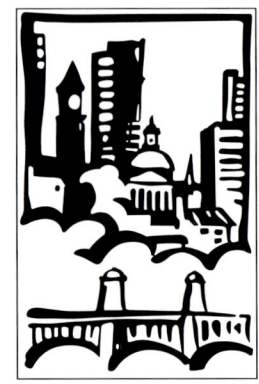

BOSTON

8

1
NCAYV

2
HEART SHARE

3
NCAYV

4
SPECIAL SINGLE ONLINE

5
DOCTORS OF THE WORLD

6
MISSION POSSIBLE MUSIC

7
MACDONALD HOUSE

8
COMBINED JEWISH PHILANTHRO-
PIES GENERAL ASSMBLY'95

1
THE WHOLE LIFE CENTER

2
GATEWAY OUTREACH

3
FARM FRESH FUNDRAISING

4
ELWYN

5
SILICON VALLEY CHARITY BALL

6
HABITAT FOR HUMANITY

7
JOBY'S HACIENDA INC

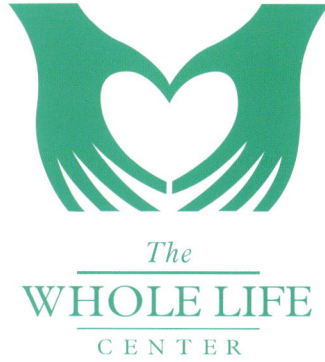

1

5

2

3

6

4

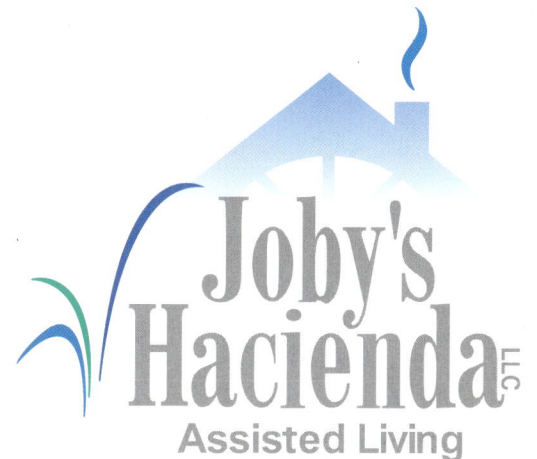

7

1

5

3

4

6

2

7

8

1
SHARE OUR STRENGTH

2
PERKS AT WORK

3
POSITIVE ABOUT DISABLED PE-
OPLE

4
JACOBS LADDER MUD

5
DEPARTMENT OF POWER

6
CORPORATE ANGEL NETWORK.INC

7
COMFORT CARE HOMES

8
UNITEDWAY OF THE BAY AREA

1
THE FISHER'S NET

2
WWW.NETAID.ORG

3
MARCH OF DIMES

4
NATIONAL LOTTERY CHARITIES
BOARD

5
CITY HARVEST

6
SKIP OF NEW YORK

7
SAN FRANCISCO FOOD BANK

1

2

5

3

6

4

7

1

CLOTHES
THE DEAL

2

TRUE VISION
FOUNDATION

3

5

6

1
AOL TIME WARNER FOUNDATION

2
CLOTHES THE DEAL

3
TRUE VISION FOUNDATION

4
REBUILDING TOGETHER

5
JOHNSON PRODUCTS INC

6
MDA TELETHON

7
MARK

4

7

1
HOPE COTTAGE

2
LUTHERAN BROTHERHOOD

3
BIG APPLE GREETER NEW YORK C-
ITY

4
HABITAT FOR HUMANITY

5
KIRLIN FOUNDATION

6
HAMILTON HOUSE

7
CITY MEALS-ON-WHEELS 20 Y-
EARS OF NOURISHING THE BODY
AND SOUL

8
SUSAN B.FOMEN FOUNDATION OF
CENTRAL NEW MEXICO

1

5

LUTHERAN
BROTHERHOOD

2

6

BigApple Greeter
New York City

3

7

Habitat for Humanity
CHARLOTTE

4

8

zoo Walk

1

Golden Hope

2

VISION 2020
THE RIGHT TO SIGHT

3

United Way

4

5

Big Apple Greeter
New York City

6

7

1
WINNSERV

2
GOLDEN HOPE

3
VISION 2020

4
UNITED WAY

5
CATHOLIC HEALTHCARE WEST

6
BIG APPLE GREETER

7
HABITAT FOR HUMANITY

1
SPECIES SURVIVAL PLAN

2
GREENING EARTH SOCIETY

3
DEUTSCHES ALTENHEIM (GERMAN HOME FOR THE AGED)

4
SIMULPROBE TECHNOLOGIES

5
EARTH SHARE

6
SPACES(SAVING AND PRESERVI-
NG AMERICAN CULTURAL ENVIR-
ONMENTS)

7
WOODLAND VILLAGE RETIREMENT
COMMUNITY

Species Survival Plan

1

4

GREENING
EARTH
SOCIETY

2

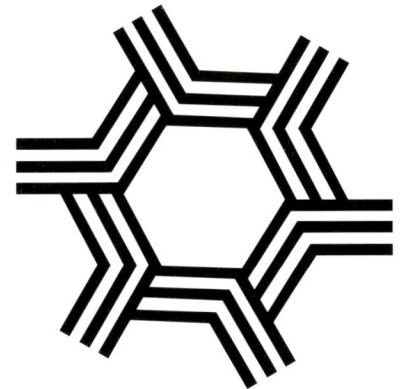

Earth Share

5

3

6

7

1

5

1
LAUGH

2
MAKE A DIFFERENCE DAY NATI-
ONNAL DAY OF DOING GOOD AN-
NUAL CHALLENGE

3
NORTHPOINTE RETIREMENT COM-
MUNITY

4
INTERNATIONAL CENTER FOR E-
THICS

5
CAL/ERP

6
CLERMONT NURSING & CONOALE-
SCENT CENTER

7
NET DAY

2

6

3

4

7

1
PRINCE SULTAN RESEARCH CEN-
TER FOR ENVIROMENT WATER &
DESSRT

2
ASIAN AMERICAN AIDS FOUNDA-
TION

3
SPOKANE PARKS FOUNDATION

4
WINSTON-SALEM FOUNDATION

5
ACCON

6
CALIFORNIA ARTS COUNCIL

7
KULSHAN COMMUNITY LAND T-
RUST

8
NATIONAL WILDLIFE FEDERA-
TION

Prince Sultan Research Center for Enviroment, Water & Dessrt

1

ACCIÓN

5

2

California

Arts Council

6

SPOKANE PARKS FOUNDATON

3

KulshanCLT

7

4

NATIONAL WILDLIFE FEDERATION®
www.nwf.org®

8

317

Your Source for Help and Hope ®

ARTHRITIS FOUNDATION®

1

2

Th + INK

3

KID'S JAM FOUNDATION

4

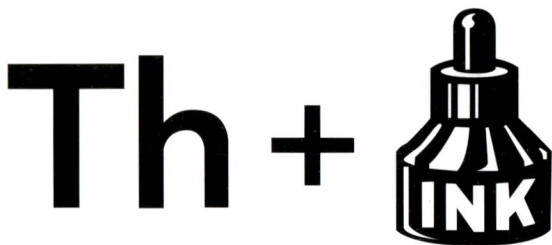

5

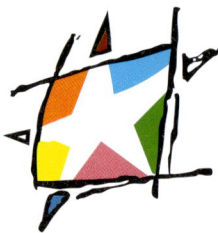

Surf Watch FOUNDATION

6

FSC

7

1
ARTHRITIS FOUNDATION

2
ROBERT F. KENNEDY FOUNDATION

3
PORTLAND SCHOOLS FOUNDATION

4
KID'S JAM FOUNDATION

5
WGBH EDUCATIONAL FOUNDATION

6
SURF WATCH FOUNDATION

7
FOREST STEWARDSHIP COUNCIL

1
THE KOREA CULTURE & ARTS F-
OUNDATION

2
NO CHILD LEFT BEHIND

3
CITY PARKS FOUNDATION CREA-
TING PROGRAMS FOR NYC PARKS

4
NATIONAL ASSOCIATION FOR A-
NNUITIES

5
TELLURIDE FOUNDATION

6
FOUNDATION FOR PARKINSON'S
RESEARCH

7
THE NEW YORK STATE HEALTH
ACCOUNTABILITY FOUNDATION

8
ARTIST TRUST

TELLURIDE FOUNDATION

5

1

NoChild
LEFT BEHIND

2

6

The New York State
Health
Accountability
Foundation

7

CityParks
Foundation
creating programs for NYC parks

3

NAVA

4

ARTIST TRUST
IT BEGINS WITH THE ARTIST

8

1

THE BREAST CANCER
RESEARCH FOUNDATION

A CURE IN OUR LIFETIME

2

5

6

3

7

The Ridgefield
Community
Foundation

4

EURO
PARTNERSHIP©

8

1
TAKE 10 CHALLENGE

2
THE BREAST CANCER RESEARCH
FOUNDATION

3
JUMP START

4
THE RIDGEFIELD COMMUNITY F-
OUNDATION

5
THE ZOO FUND

6
THE MS FOUNDATION

7
JUMP START

8
EURO PARTNER SHIP